holiday baking

JG PRESS

Treats filled with cheer
for a magical time of year

For general information on our other products and services or to obtain technical support please contact our Customer Care Department within the U.S. at 800-762-2974, outside the U.S. at 317-572-3993 or fax 317-572-4002.

Wiley also publishes its books in a variety of electronic formats. Some content that appears in print may not be available in electronic books. For more information about Wiley products, visit our web site at www.wiley.com.

Wiley Bicentennial Logo: Richard J. Pacifico

Library of Congress Cataloging-in-Publication Data:

Pillsbury holiday baking / Pillsbury editors.

    p. cm.

Includes index.

ISBN: 978-1-57215-809-2 (cloth)

1. Baking. 2. Holiday cookery. I. C.A. Pillsbury and Company.

TX765.P537 2007

641.8'65--dc22

        2006025131

Manufactured in China

10 9 8 7 6 5 4 3 2 1

General Mills

Publisher, Books and Magazines: Sheila Burke

Manager, Cookbook Publishing: Lois Tlusty

Editor: Lori Fox

Food Editor: Lola Whalen

Recipe Development and Testing: Pillsbury Kitchens

Photography: General Mills Photography Studios and Image Library

Photographer: Val Bourassa

Food Stylists: Carol Grones, Susan Brosious

Wiley Publishing, Inc.

Publisher: Natalie Chapman

Executive Editor: Anne Ficklen

Editor: Adam Kowit

Production Editors: Angela Riley and Michael Olivo

Cover Design: Paul Dinovo and Suzanne Sunwoo

Art Director: Tai Blanche

Photography Art Direction: Lynne Dolan

Manufacturing Manager: Kevin Watt

Home of the Pillsbury Bake-Off® Contest

Pillsbury

Our recipes have been tested in the Pillsbury Kitchens and meet our standards of easy preparation, reliability and great taste.

For more great recipes visit pillsbury.com

Cover photo: Peppermint Whoopie Pies, page 195

Welcome . . .

There's something magical about the **holidays**. Frosting cookies or filling a pie creates that warm **fuzzy feeling** you only get this time of year. And there's something about a gift of **home-baked** food that's just so heartfelt. The simplest tin of cookies or bars (maybe wrapped in a **pretty ribbon**) is like a little **box of love**.

We want to help you sprinkle your **holidays** with cheer and fill them with warmth. It's almost as easy as turning on your oven—really! We've filled our recipes with **super-easy** shortcuts and lots of **fun ideas**—so you'll soon be adding your own **special touches** with colorful decorations, icings and more.

If you have kids, flip through the pages for ideas like the totally cute Bugs in a Blanket (perfect for a Halloween **party**) and cookie ornaments (one for the tree, one for me . . .). To add the "**wow**" factor, there are **cakes** shaped like gingerbread men, **pies** topped with snowflakes and tons of colorful layered bars.

However you **celebrate** the holidays, baking is a fun, easy way to **share** moments that become fond **memories**. Wishing you an icing-coated smile and a **happy holiday season**!

Warmly,

The Pillsbury Editors

contents

bake shop storage

storing unbaked cookie dough

Unbaked cookie dough can be tightly covered and put in the fridge up to 3 days before baking. If the dough is too stiff to work with, let it stand up to 2 hours at room temperature until it's pliable.

To freeze, wrap batches of unbaked cookie dough in waxed paper, plastic wrap or foil, then put in resealable plastic freezer bags or containers; label with date and freeze up to 6 months. Dough can also be shaped into rolls, rectangles or individual cookies before freezing. Freeze rolls and rectangles as directed above. Freeze individual drops of cookie dough on cookie sheets; when completely frozen, store as directed above. Don't freeze meringue, macaroon mixtures or any dough using beaten egg whites. The egg whites break down during freezing, and the cookies won't bake correctly.

Before baking, thaw frozen dough in the refrigerator at least 8 hours. If it's still too stiff, let it stand up to 2 hours at room temperature until it's easier to work with.

storing baked cookies and bars

Store different flavors of cookies in separate containers, or they will pick up the flavors of the other cookies.

Store the same kind of cookies together—crisp with crisp, soft with soft, chewy with chewy and so on. If you mix crisp cookies with soft or chewy cookies, the crisp cookies will get soft.

Store crisp cookies at room temperature in a loosely covered container.

Store soft or chewy cookies at room temperature in resealable plastic bags or tightly covered containers.

Store frosted or decorated cookies between layers of waxed paper, plastic wrap or foil. Let frosting set or harden before storing.

Store most bars right in the baking pan, tightly covered.

Freeze cookies and bars in freezer containers with tight-fitting lids; label with date. Freeze unfrosted cookies and bars up to 1 year and frosted cookies and bars up to 3 months. Don't freeze meringue, custard-filled or cream-filled cookies. Freeze delicate frosted or decorated cookies between layers of waxed paper, plastic wrap or foil.

Thaw most cookies and bars, covered, in the container at room temperature 1 to 2 hours. Dense, heavy bars might take a little longer. For crisp cookies, thaw uncovered so they don't get soft.

secrets for mailing holiday goodies

Homemade cookies and bars are the greatest, especially when sent to family and friends away from home. College students especially love getting a gift of home baking! To assure the gifts from your heart arrive in one piece instead of crumbs, follow these tips:

getting ready

Bake and freeze bars in disposable foil pans for ready-made gift platters. Look for pans with plastic lids.

Cool all baked goods completely before wrapping and freezing. Freeze frosted cookies uncovered in a single layer until firm before storing or packaging.

When mailing more than one kind of cookie or bar, wrap each kind separately so your sugar cookies don't taste like ginger cookies or your brownies don't taste like pumpkin bars.

Wrap loaves of bread tightly in plastic wrap.

let's pack

Pack treats in a strong, corrugated cardboard box, metal or plastic container with lid or decorative container with lid. Going with just the box? Line it with plastic wrap, waxed paper or foil because cookies can absorb a cardboard flavor from boxes.

Pack baked goods in the container between layers of crumpled waxed paper or bubble wrap, starting and ending with a cushioning layer.

Pack the container full enough to prevent baked goodies from shifting.

Place metal, plastic or decorative containers in a strong, corrugated cardboard box with rigid sides. The box should be big enough to leave several inches all around for cushioning. Cushion box with crumpled newspaper, bubble wrap, foam pellets or shredded paper.

Oops! Don't forget to put your card inside before sealing the box.

Seal the box tightly with shipping or strapping tape. Address the box clearly, and cover the address with transparent tape to protect it from blurring. Mark the box FRAGILE and PERISHABLE.

happy
halloween

Peanut Butter Autumn Spotlights • Secret-Center Cookie Cups • Meringue Ghosts • Candy Corn– and Peanut-Topped Brownies • Frankenstein Cake • The Great Pumpkin Cake • Apple Pecan Layer Cake with Brown Butter Frosting • Pumpkin Pound Cake with Walnut Sauce • Halloween Cupcake Trio • Individual Cheesy Apple Crisps • Gingerbread Bran Muffins • Crispy Bat Snacks and "Appledy-Goop" • Halloween Cookie Pizza • Moldy Bones with Ghoulish Dip • Wart-Topped Quesadilla Wedges • Bugs in a Blanket

peanut butter autumn spotlights

Prep Time: **1 hour**	Start to Finish: **1 hour**	3 $^1/_2$ dozen cookies

1 box (1 lb 2.25 oz) yellow cake
   mix with pudding

$^1/_2$ cup peanut butter

$^1/_4$ cup butter or margarine,
   softened

$^1/_4$ cup water

2 eggs

1 cup candy-coated peanut
   butter pieces

1 Heat oven to 350°F. In large bowl, beat cake mix, peanut butter, butter, water and eggs with electric mixer on low speed until well blended. Stir in candy pieces. Drop by rounded teaspoonfuls 2 inches apart onto ungreased cookie sheets.

2 Bake 8 to 12 minutes or until light golden brown. Immediately remove from cookie sheets.

Kick up the holiday theme by looking for seasonally available bags of orange and black candies, or buy several regular bags and use only the orange and dark brown candies. If you can't find candy-coated peanut butter pieces, then use candy-coated chocolate candies.

High Altitude (3500–6500 ft): Bake 10 to 14 minutes.

1 Cookie: Calories 110 (Calories from Fat 45); Total Fat 5g (Saturated Fat 1.5g; Trans Fat 0g); Cholesterol 15mg; Sodium 115mg; Total Carbohydrate 13g (Dietary Fiber 0g; Sugars 8g); Protein 2g % Daily Value: Vitamin A 0%; Vitamin C 0%; Calcium 2%; Iron 0% Exchanges: $^1/_2$ Starch, $^1/_2$ Other Carbohydrate, 1 Fat Carbohydrate Choices: 1

secret-center cookie cups

extra easy

| Prep Time: **55 minutes** | Start to Finish: **1 hour 10 minutes** | 3 dozen cookies |

1 roll (16.5 oz) refrigerated
  peanut butter cookies

36 miniature bars (about 1 inch
  square) chocolate-covered
  peanut, caramel and nougat
  candy, unwrapped

36 miniature paper or foil baking
  cups (1 $^1/_4$-inch diameter)

$^3/_4$ cup chocolate creamy
  ready-to-spread frosting
  (from 1-lb container)

1 Heat oven to 375°F. For each cookie cup, wrap heaping teaspoonful cookie dough around 1 candy bar, enclosing it almost completely and forming ball. Place in paper baking cup; place cups 1 inch apart on ungreased cookie sheets.

2 Bake 8 to 12 minutes or until golden brown. Centers of cookies will sink slightly. Cool 1 minute; remove from cookie sheets. Cool completely, about 15 minutes.

3 Spoon frosting into pastry bag fitted with star tip. Pipe frosting on top of each cookie cup.

Don't worry if you don't have a pastry bag. Just put the frosting in a resealable food-storage plastic bag and snip off a very small section of the corner (no more than $^1/_4$ inch wide); squeeze dollops of frosting on the top of each cookie cup. Or, use a spoon to add the dollops of frosting.

High Altitude (3500–6500 ft):
No change.

1 Cookie: Calories 120 (Calories from Fat 50); Total Fat 6g (Saturated Fat 2g; Trans Fat 1g); Cholesterol 0mg; Sodium 100mg; Total Carbohydrate 16g (Dietary Fiber 0g; Sugars 12g); Protein 2g % Daily Value: Vitamin A 0%; Vitamin C 0%; Calcium 0%; Iron 0% Exchanges: $^1/_2$ Starch, $^1/_2$ Other Carbohydrate, 1 Fat Carbohydrate Choices: 1

meringue ghosts

2 egg whites

$^1/_8$ teaspoon cream of tartar

$^1/_2$ cup sugar

$^1/_4$ teaspoon vanilla

1 $^1/_4$ teaspoons miniature
  semisweet chocolate chips

1   Heat oven to 200°F. Line 2 large cookie sheets with parchment paper. In small bowl, beat egg whites and cream of tartar with electric mixer on medium speed until foamy. Gradually add sugar, 1 tablespoon at a time, beating on high speed until meringue is very stiff and glossy, and sugar is dissolved. Reduce speed to low; beat in vanilla just until well mixed.

2   Use disposable decorating bag or gallon-size resealable food-storage plastic bag with $^1/_2$-inch hole cut in bottom corner. Spoon meringue into bag; twist top to partially close bag.

3   Squeeze bag to pipe meringue into 4-inch ghost shapes on cookie sheets. Place 3 chocolate chips on each ghost for eyes and mouth.

4   Place cookie sheets on center racks in oven; bake 2 hours. Place parchment paper and cookies on cooling rack. Cool completely, about 10 minutes. Remove cookies from parchment paper.

Make frosted cupcakes even more fun by topping each with one of these cute ghosts.

High Altitude (3500–6500 ft):
No change.

1 Cookie: Calories 20 (Calories from Fat 0); Total Fat 0g (Saturated Fat 0g; Trans Fat 0g); Cholesterol 0mg; Sodium 0mg; Total Carbohydrate 4g (Dietary Fiber 0g; Sugars 4g); Protein 0g % Daily Value: Vitamin A 0%; Vitamin C 0%; Calcium 0%; Iron 0% Exchanges: Free Carbohydrate Choices: 0

candy corn– and peanut-topped brownies

Prep Time: **15 minutes**	Start to Finish: **2 hours**	36 brownies

BASE

1 box (1 lb 3.8 oz) fudge
    brownie mix

$1/_2$ cup vegetable oil

$1/_4$ cup water

2 eggs

2 cups miniature marshmallows

TOPPING

$1/_2$ cup packed brown sugar

$1/_2$ cup light corn syrup

$1/_2$ cup creamy peanut butter

2 cups sweetened squares
    rice cereal

1 $1/_2$ cups salted peanuts

1 cup candy corn

1 Heat oven to 350°F. Grease bottom only of 13 × 9-inch pan with shortening. In medium bowl, stir brownie mix, oil, water and eggs with spoon until well blended. Spread in pan.

2 Bake 28 to 30 minutes or until toothpick inserted 2 inches from side of pan comes out almost clean.

3 Immediately sprinkle marshmallows evenly over warm base; bake 1 to 2 minutes longer or until marshmallows just begin to puff. Cool while making topping.

4 In 3-quart saucepan, cook brown sugar and corn syrup over medium heat, stirring constantly, until mixture boils. Remove from heat. Stir in peanut butter until well blended. Stir in cereal, peanuts and candy corn until coated. Immediately spoon warm topping over marshmallows, spreading to cover. Cool completely, about 1 $1/_4$ hours. For brownies, cut into 6 rows by 6 rows.

Fun food gifts aren't just for Christmas! Line a plastic or ceramic pumpkin with orange and black or Halloween-theme print tissue paper. Arrange individually wrapped brownies in lined container.

High Altitude (3500–6500 ft): Follow High Altitude directions on brownie mix box for cake-like brownies.

1 Brownie: Calories 220 (Calories from Fat 80); Total Fat 9g (Saturated Fat 1.5g; Trans Fat 0g); Cholesterol 10mg; Sodium 150mg; Total Carbohydrate 31g (Dietary Fiber 0g; Sugars 22g); Protein 3g % Daily Value: Vitamin A 0%; Vitamin C 0%; Calcium 2%; Iron 8% Exchanges: 1 Starch, 1 Other Carbohydrate, 1 $1/_2$ Fat Carbohydrate Choices: 2

ghoulish ideas for fun food

Scare up some great fun for Halloween, America's most celebrated holiday! Invite neighborhood kids in for a treat—not tricks. Creating a festive table with loads of color and some "yucky" stuff is an easy way to get lots of giggles and smiles.

Decorate the table with bright orange, yellow, green and black disposable place settings and tablecloth. Mix and match—kids like zany color combinations.

Scatter tablecloth with "sweet and spooky" confetti-like candy corn or other brightly colored candy and spooky little skeletons, spiders, and rubber eyeballs.

Miniature fresh pumpkins make great place cards. Write names on pumpkins with permanent marker; let dry. Brush around name with glue; sprinkle with glitter or colored sugar and let dry.

"Yuck it up" with wormy, googly-eye napkin rings! Use 1 pipe cleaner, 2 googly eyes and 2 to 3 gummy candy worms per napkin. Glue 1 googly eye on each end of pipe cleaner; let dry. Roll up a colored paper napkin and put gummy candy worms lengthwise down length of napkin; secure with pipe cleaner, googly eyes facing up.

frankenstein cake

Prep Time: **20 minutes**   Start to Finish: **2 hours 5 minutes**   12 servings

1 box (1 lb 2.25 oz) white cake
mix with pudding

1 1/4 cups water

1/3 cup vegetable oil

3 egg whites

1/4 teaspoon green paste icing
color (not liquid food color)

1 container (1 lb) vanilla creamy
ready-to-spread frosting

1/2 cup chocolate creamy
ready-to-spread frosting
(from 1-lb container)

1 large marshmallow

1 large orange gumdrop

2 large red gumdrops

Candy corn

Chocolate candies

1 Heat oven to 350°F (if using dark or nonstick pans, heat oven to 325°F). Spray bottom only of 13 × 9-inch pan with cooking spray. In large bowl, beat cake mix, water, oil, egg whites and 1/8 teaspoon paste icing color with electric mixer on low speed 30 seconds. Beat on medium speed 2 minutes, scraping bowl occasionally. Pour batter into pan. Bake 26 to 31 minutes or until toothpick inserted in center comes out clean. Cool completely, about 1 hour.

2 Stir remaining 1/8 teaspoon paste icing color into vanilla frosting until well blended. Frost cooled cake with green frosting.

3 Spoon chocolate frosting into small plastic bag; seal bag. Cut small hole in one bottom corner of bag. Squeeze bag to pipe frosting onto 2 to 4 inches of one short end of cake to resemble hair around face. (See photo.)

4 Cut marshmallow in half crosswise; place on cake for eyes. Shape orange gumdrop for nose. Cut one red gumdrop in half crosswise; place on top of marshmallows for irises of eyes. Use chocolate frosting to add pupils to eyes, and big scar with stitches across forehead and cheek. Flatten remaining red gumdrop for mouth; place on cake and add candy corn teeth. Make bolts with chocolate candies.

High Altitude (3500–6500 ft): Follow High Altitude directions on cake mix box.

1 Serving: Calories 470 (Calories from Fat 190); Total Fat 21g (Saturated Fat 5g; Trans Fat 4.5g); Cholesterol 0mg; Sodium 430mg; Total Carbohydrate 68g (Dietary Fiber 0g; Sugars 49g); Protein 3g % Daily Value: Vitamin A 0%; Vitamin C 0%; Calcium 4%; Iron 6% Exchanges: 1 Starch, 3 1/2 Other Carbohydrate, 4 Fat Carbohydrate Choices: 4 1/2

Paste food color is much more vibrant and intense than liquid food color, and doesn't thin out frosting as much as liquids do. Look for paste food color in the cake decorating section of department or craft stores.

the great pumpkin cake

CAKE

2 boxes (1 lb 2.25 oz each)
  yellow cake mix with pudding

2 1/2 cups water

2/3 cup vegetable oil

6 eggs

FROSTING AND DECORATION

1/2 teaspoon orange paste icing
  color (not liquid food color)

2 containers (1 lb each) vanilla
  creamy ready-to-spread
  frosting

1 flat-bottom ice cream cone

1/2 cup dark chocolate creamy
  ready-to-spread frosting
  (from 1-lb container)

2 green candy-colored chocolate
  baking bits

2 pieces candy corn

4 lime wedge candy jellies

1 Heat oven to 350°F (if using dark or nonstick pans, heat oven to 325°F). Grease 12-cup fluted tube (bundt cake) pan with shortening; lightly flour. In large bowl, beat 1 cake mix, 1 1/4 cups water, 1/3 cup oil and 3 eggs with electric mixer on low speed 30 seconds or until blended. Beat on medium speed 2 minutes, scraping bowl occasionally. Pour batter into pan.

2 Bake 39 to 44 minutes or until toothpick inserted in center comes out clean. Cool cake in pan 15 minutes. Remove from pan; place on cooling rack. Cool completely, about 1 hour. Repeat for second cake, using remaining cake mix, water, oil and eggs.

3 Stir 1/4 teaspoon of the orange paste icing color into each container of vanilla frosting. To make pumpkin shape, place 1 cake, rounded side down, on serving plate (if necessary, trim cakes to form flat surfaces). Spread top with 1/3 cup orange frosting. Place second cake, rounded side up, on top of first cake. Frost both cakes with remaining orange frosting.

4 Frost outside of ice cream cone with 1/3 cup of the chocolate frosting. In small resealable food-storage plastic bag, place remaining cup chocolate frosting; seal bag. Cut tiny hole in one bottom corner of bag. Squeeze bag to draw eyes, nose and mouth on pumpkin with frosting. Add baking bits for irises of eyes and candy corn for teeth.

5 Insert frosted cone in center of cake to form pumpkin stem. With knife, cut leaf shapes from fruit snack roll; place near stem. To serve cake, cut slices from top cake before cutting bottom cake.

High Altitude (3500–6500 ft): Follow High Altitude directions on cake mix box.

1 Serving: Calories 440 (Calories from Fat 180); Total Fat 20g (Saturated Fat 5g; Trans Fat 4.5g); Cholesterol 55mg; Sodium 410mg; Total Carbohydrate 63g (Dietary Fiber 0g; Sugars 48g); Protein 3g % Daily Value: Vitamin A 0%; Vitamin C 0%; Calcium 6%; Iron 6% Exchanges: 1 Starch, 3 Other Carbohydrate, 4 Fat Carbohydrate Choices: 4

apple pecan layer cake with brown butter frosting

Prep Time: **35 minutes**   Start to Finish: **2 hours 10 minutes**   12 servings

CAKE

2 1/2 cups all-purpose flour

2 cups granulated sugar

1 teaspoon baking powder

1 teaspoon baking soda

1 teaspoon salt

1 teaspoon ground cinnamon

1 1/2 cups applesauce

3/4 cup vegetable oil

2 eggs

1/2 cup chopped pecans

BROWN BUTTER FROSTING

1/2 cup butter (do not use
    margarine)

4 1/2 cups powdered sugar

6 to 8 tablespoons apple juice

1 Heat oven to 350°F. Grease two 9-inch round cake pans with shortening; lightly flour. In large bowl, mix flour, granulated sugar, baking powder, baking soda, salt and cinnamon. Add applesauce, oil and eggs; beat with electric mixer on low speed until moistened. Beat on high speed 2 minutes. Stir in pecans. Pour batter into pans.

2 Bake 30 to 40 minutes or until toothpick inserted in center comes out clean. Cool 10 minutes; remove from pans. Cool completely.

3 In small heavy saucepan, brown butter over medium heat, stirring constantly, until light golden brown. Remove from heat; cool completely. In large bowl, beat browned butter, powdered sugar and 4 tablespoons of the apple juice with electric mixer on low speed until moistened. Continue beating until well blended, adding additional apple juice until desired spreading consistency. Fill and frost cake.

While the kids are enjoying their own Halloween treats, the adults can indulge in a slice of this moist spice cake with brown butter frosting. Serve with rum-raisin or cinnamon ice cream and hot apple cider.

High Altitude (3500–6500 ft): Heat oven to 375°F. Decrease granulated sugar to 1 3/4 cups. Bake 25 to 35 minutes.

1 Serving: Calories 670 (Calories from Fat 230); Total Fat 26g (Saturated Fat 7g; Trans Fat 0g); Cholesterol 55mg; Sodium 410mg; Total Carbohydrate 106g (Dietary Fiber 2g; Sugars 83g); Protein 4g % Daily Value: Vitamin A 6%; Vitamin C 0%; Calcium 4%; Iron 10% Exchanges: 1 Starch, 6 Other Carbohydrate, 5 Fat Carbohydrate Choices: 7

pumpkin pound cake with walnut sauce

Prep Time: **30 minutes**   Start to Finish: **2 hours 55 minutes**   16 servings

CAKE

2 ³/₄ cups granulated sugar

1 ¹/₂ cups butter or margarine, softened

1 teaspoon vanilla

6 eggs

3 cups all-purpose flour

¹/₂ teaspoon baking powder

¹/₂ teaspoon salt

³/₄ teaspoon ground cinnamon

¹/₂ teaspoon ground ginger

¹/₄ teaspoon ground cloves

1 cup canned pumpkin (not pumpkin pie mix)

SAUCE

1 cup packed brown sugar

¹/₂ cup whipping cream

¹/₄ cup dark corn syrup

2 tablespoons butter or margarine

Dash salt

¹/₂ teaspoon vanilla

¹/₂ cup chopped walnuts

1 Heat oven to 350°F. Generously grease 12-cup fluted tube (bundt cake) pan with shortening; lightly flour. In large bowl, beat granulated sugar and 1 ¹/₂ cups butter until light and fluffy. Add 1 teaspoon vanilla; beat in 1 egg at a time until well blended. In small bowl, mix flour, baking powder, ¹/₂ teaspoon salt, the cinnamon, ginger and cloves. Alternately add dry ingredients and pumpkin to butter mixture, beating well after each addition. Pour batter into pan.

2 Bake 60 to 70 minutes or until toothpick inserted in center comes out clean. Cool 15 minutes; invert onto serving plate. Cool completely.

3 In medium saucepan, heat brown sugar, whipping cream, corn syrup, 2 tablespoons butter and dash salt to boiling over medium heat, stirring constantly. Reduce heat to low; simmer 5 minutes, stirring constantly. Remove from heat; stir in ¹/₂ teaspoon vanilla and the walnuts. Serve warm sauce over cake. Refrigerate any remaining sauce.

Make and freeze this yummy cake and sauce up to 1 month ahead of time. Just before serving, heat the sauce in the microwave. If you'd like, serve with a dollop of whipped cream, too.

High Altitude (3500–6500 ft): Heat oven to 375°F. Decrease granulated sugar to 2 ¹/₂ cups. Bake 50 to 60 minutes.

1 Serving: Calories 540 (Calories from Fat 230); Total Fat 26g (Saturated Fat 14g; Trans Fat 1g); Cholesterol 135mg; Sodium 270mg; Total Carbohydrate 72g (Dietary Fiber 1g; Sugars 51g); Protein 6g % Daily Value: Vitamin A 60%; Vitamin C 0%; Calcium 6%; Iron 10% Exchanges: 1 ¹/₂ Starch, 3 ¹/₂ Other Carbohydrate, 5 Fat Carbohydrate Choices: 5

halloween cupcake trio

Prep Time: **1 hour**   Start to Finish: **1 hour**   24 cupcakes

CUPCAKES

1 container (1 lb) vanilla creamy
   ready-to-spread frosting
1/4 teaspoon orange paste icing
   color (not liquid food color)
24 unfrosted cupcakes

SPIDER WEB TOPPING

Black decorating gel
8 clean plastic spider finger rings

EYEBALL TOPPING

2 tablespoons vanilla creamy
   ready-to-spread frosting
   (from 1-lb container)
8 miniature candy-coated
   chocolate baking bits
8 miniature semisweet
   chocolate chips
Red decorating gel

GRAVE TOPPING

Black decorating gel
8 oval creme-filled peanut butter
   sandwich cookies
1/4 cup chocolate cookie crumbs
8 candy pumpkins

1 In small bowl, place 2 tablespoons of the frosting; set aside. Stir orange icing color into remaining frosting in container until well blended and no streaks remain. Frost cupcakes.

2 To make spider web topping on cupcakes, use black decorating gel to draw coil covering top of each frosted cupcake. Drag toothpick through coil from the center out, creating a web. Press 1 spider ring onto each "web."

3 To make eyeball topping on cupcakes, drop about 1/2 teaspoon reserved vanilla frosting onto each frosted cupcake. Lightly press 1 baking bit in center of each. Attach 1 miniature chocolate chip to center of each baking bit with tiny dot of frosting. Use red decorating gel to draw red squiggly lines radiating around edge of white frosting to resemble veins.

4 To make grave topping on cupcakes, use black decorating gel to write an "epitaph" on one end of each cookie. Press cookies into cupcakes to form "gravestones." Sprinkle cookie crumbs around each "gravestone." Place candy pumpkin to one side of gravestone.

Here's an easy decorating idea for the table or serving platter. Feed orange, black and green tissue paper through a paper shredder to create your own confetti; arrange some confetti loosely on a serving platter before adding the cupcakes, or scatter it on the table.

High Altitude (3500–6500 ft): No change.

1 Cupcake: Calories 200 (Calories from Fat 80); Total Fat 9g (Saturated Fat 2.5g; Trans Fat 2g); Cholesterol 15mg; Sodium 170mg; Total Carbohydrate 29g (Dietary Fiber 0g; Sugars 22g); Protein 1g % Daily Value: Vitamin A 0%; Vitamin C 0%; Calcium 0%; Iron 2% Exchanges: 2 Other Carbohydrate, 2 Fat Carbohydrate Choices: 2

individual cheesy apple crisps

Prep Time: **30 minutes**	Start to Finish: **55 minutes**	6 servings

3 slices (0.75 oz each) Cheddar
cheese product

4 cups sliced peeled apples
(4 medium)

$^1/_2$ cup granulated sugar

$^1/_2$ teaspoon ground cinnamon

1 tablespoon lemon juice

$^1/_2$ cup all-purpose flour

$^1/_2$ cup old-fashioned oats

$^1/_4$ cup packed brown sugar

$^1/_4$ cup butter or margarine

1 Heat oven to 375°F. Using holiday-shaped cookie cutters, cut 2 shapes from each cheese slice. Cover; refrigerate. Chop remaining cheese scraps; set aside.

2 In large bowl, toss apples, granulated sugar, cinnamon and lemon juice to coat apple slices. In medium bowl, mix flour, oats and brown sugar. Using pastry blender or fork, cut in butter until mixture is consistency of coarse crumbs. Spoon apple mixture into each of 6 ungreased 6-ounce custard cups. Top with chopped cheese; sprinkle with crumb mixture. Place cups in 15 × 10 × 1-inch pan.

3 Bake 18 to 25 minutes or until apples are tender and topping is golden brown. Top each with cheese cutout; bake 1 to 2 minutes longer or until cheese begins to melt.

This down-home dessert is baked in individual 6-ounce custard cups. Personalize each by creating festive cheese cutouts, in holiday shapes, for the finishing touch.

High Altitude (3500–6500 ft):
Bake 23 to 28 minutes.

1 Serving: Calories 320 (Calories from Fat 110); Total Fat 12g (Saturated Fat 7g; Trans Fat 0.5g); Cholesterol 30mg; Sodium 125mg; Total Carbohydrate 48g (Dietary Fiber 2g; Sugars 33g); Protein 5g % Daily Value: Vitamin A 8%; Vitamin C 4%; Calcium 8%; Iron 6% Exchanges: 1 Starch, $^1/_2$ Fruit, 1 $^1/_2$ Other Carbohydrate, 2 $^1/_2$ Fat Carbohydrate Choices: 3

gingerbread bran muffins

| Prep Time: **20 minutes** | Start to Finish: **45 minutes** | 12 muffins |

MUFFINS

1 egg

$^1/_4$ cup sugar

1 cup buttermilk*

$^1/_3$ cup vegetable oil

$^1/_4$ cup molasses

1 $^1/_2$ cups bran cereal shreds
   (do not use bran flakes)

1 cup all-purpose flour

1 $^1/_2$ teaspoons baking powder

$^1/_2$ teaspoon baking soda

$^1/_2$ teaspoon ground ginger

$^1/_4$ teaspoon salt

$^1/_4$ teaspoon ground cinnamon

$^1/_4$ teaspoon ground cloves

TOPPING

2 tablespoons sugar

1 In medium bowl, lightly beat egg. Add $^1/_4$ cup sugar, the buttermilk, oil and molasses; beat well with wire whisk. Stir in cereal. Let stand 10 minutes.

2 In small bowl, mix all remaining muffin ingredients. Add to bran mixture; mix well. Bake immediately, or cover and refrigerate 8 hours or overnight.

3 Heat oven to 375°F. Place paper baking cup in each of 12 regular-size muffin cups. Divide batter evenly among muffin cups. Sprinkle each with $^1/_2$ teaspoon sugar.

4 Bake 20 to 25 minutes or until tops spring back when touched lightly. Remove from pan. Serve warm or cool.

* To substitute for buttermilk, use 1 tablespoon vinegar or lemon juice plus milk to make 1 cup.

For more whole grain goodness, $^1/_2$ cup whole wheat flour can be substituted for $^1/_2$ cup of the all-purpose flour.

High Altitude (3500–6500 ft):
No change.

1 Muffin: Calories 180 (Calories from Fat 70); Total Fat 7g (Saturated Fat 1.5g; Trans Fat 0g); Cholesterol 20mg; Sodium 220mg; Total Carbohydrate 27g (Dietary Fiber 4g; Sugars 11g); Protein 3g % Daily Value: Vitamin A 0%; Vitamin C 0%; Calcium 10%; Iron 10% Exchanges: $^1/_2$ Starch, 1 $^1/_2$ Other Carbohydrate, 1 Fat Carbohydrate Choices: 2

crispy bat snacks and "appledy-goop"

Prep Time: **15 minutes**   Start to Finish: **30 minutes**   4 servings ($^1/_4$ cup dip and 3 bat snacks each)

6 flour tortillas (6 inch)

Cooking spray

$^1/_2$ cup apple butter

$^1/_3$ cup crunchy peanut butter

2 teaspoons apple juice or
   apple cider

1 tablespoon chopped peanuts

1 Heat oven to 350°F. With 3-inch bat-shaped cookie cutter or knife, cut tortillas into bat shapes. Place shapes and large scraps on ungreased cookie sheets. Spray both sides of shapes and scraps with cooking spray.

2 Bake 8 to 10 minutes or until golden brown and crisp. Cool completely, about 15 minutes.

3 Meanwhile, in small bowl, mix remaining ingredients except peanuts. Sprinkle dip with peanuts. Serve dip with bat snacks.

Pack this dip with a few bat snacks for a tasty Halloween lunch box surprise! Look for apple butter in the jam and jelly section of the store.

High Altitude (3500–6500 ft):
No change.

1 Serving: Calories 350 (Calories from Fat 150); Total Fat 16g (Saturated Fat 3g; Trans Fat 0.5g); Cholesterol 0mg; Sodium 300mg; Total Carbohydrate 43g (Dietary Fiber 3g; Sugars 18g); Protein 9g % Daily Value: Vitamin A 0%; Vitamin C 0%; Calcium 6%; Iron 10% Exchanges: 2 Starch, 1 Other Carbohydrate, $^1/_2$ High-Fat Meat, 2 Fat Carbohydrate Choices: 3

halloween cookie pizza

Prep Time: **15 minutes**   Start to Finish: **1 hour 5 minutes**   16 servings

1 roll (16.5 oz) refrigerated
    sugar cookies
$^1/_2$ cup creamy peanut butter
1 cup candy corn
$^1/_2$ cup raisins
$^1/_4$ cup vanilla creamy
    ready-to-spread frosting
    (from 1-lb container)

1 Heat oven to 350°F. Line 12-inch pizza pan with foil; grease foil with shortening. Cut cookie dough into $^1/_4$-inch slices; arrange evenly in pan. With floured fingers, press slices to form crust.

2 Bake 16 to 20 minutes or until deep golden brown. Cool completely, about 30 minutes.

3 Use foil to lift crust from pan. Carefully remove foil from crust; place crust on serving platter or tray. Spread peanut butter over crust. Sprinkle candy corn and raisins evenly over top.

4 In small microwavable bowl, microwave frosting on High 10 to 15 seconds or until thin and drizzling consistency. Drizzle frosting over cookie pizza. Cut into wedges or squares.

If your kids don't like candy corn and raisins, substitute any small favorite candies.

High Altitude (3500–6500 ft):
No change.

1 Serving: Calories 250 (Calories from Fat 100); Total Fat 11g (Saturated Fat 2.5g; Trans Fat 1.5g); Cholesterol 10mg; Sodium 130mg; Total Carbohydrate 37g (Dietary Fiber 0g; Sugars 25g); Protein 3g % Daily Value: Vitamin A 0%; Vitamin C 0%; Calcium 0%; Iron 6% Exchanges: 1 Starch, 1 $^1/_2$ Other Carbohydrate, 2 Fat Carbohydrate Choices: 2 $^1/_2$

moldy bones with ghoulish dip

Prep Time: **10 minutes**   Start to Finish: **25 minutes**   6 servings (2 tablespoons dip and 1 breadstick each)

1 can (7 oz) refrigerated original
  breadsticks (6 breadsticks)

1 egg white, beaten

1 tablespoon grated Parmesan
  cheese

$^1/_2$ teaspoon dried basil leaves

1 can (8 oz) pizza sauce, heated

1 Heat oven to 375°F. Spray cookie sheet with cooking spray. Unroll dough; separate at perforations into 6 breadsticks. Roll each until 12 inches long. Loosely tie knot in both ends of each breadstick; place on cookie sheet (do not twist).

2 Brush breadsticks with egg white. Sprinkle with cheese and basil.

3 Bake 12 to 14 minutes or until golden brown. Serve warm "bones" with warm pizza sauce for dipping.

Prepare a bewitching menu card for tonight's delights: Moldy Bones with Ghoulish Dip, Witch's Hair with Goblin Eyeballs (spaghetti and meatballs), Tossed Garden Weeds (green salad).

High Altitude (3500–6500 ft):
No change.

1 Serving: Calories 160 (Calories from Fat 25); Total Fat 3g (Saturated Fat 0.5g; Trans Fat 0.5g); Cholesterol 0mg; Sodium 560mg; Total Carbohydrate 28g (Dietary Fiber 0g; Sugars 5g); Protein 6g % Daily Value: Vitamin A 0%; Vitamin C 0%; Calcium 0%; Iron 10% Exchanges: 2 Starch Carbohydrate Choices: 2

wart-topped quesadilla wedges

Prep Time: **10 minutes**   Start to Finish: **30 minutes**   8 servings (2 wedges each)

Cooking spray

4 flour tortillas (8 inch)

$^1/_2$ cup refrigerated original barbeque sauce with shredded pork (from 18-oz container)

2 teaspoons dill pickle relish

$^1/_2$ cup shredded American-Cheddar cheese blend (2 oz)

4 teaspoons shredded American-Cheddar cheese blend ($^1/_3$ oz)

8 pitted large ripe or green olives, cut in half lengthwise

1 Heat oven to 375°F. Spray cookie sheet with cooking spray. Place 2 tortillas on cookie sheet. Spread half of the barbeque sauce with pork over each tortilla. Sprinkle half of the pickle relish over each. Top with $^1/_2$ cup cheese and remaining tortillas. Spray top of each with cooking spray.

2 Bake 10 to 12 minutes or until tortillas are lightly browned and filling is hot.

3 Immediately drop 4 teaspoons cheese by $^1/_4$ teaspoonfuls around edges of quesadillas, spacing evenly and making 8 piles of cheese on each. Top each pile of cheese with 1 olive half to resemble wart.

4 Bake about 1 minute longer or until cheese is melted. Let stand 5 minutes before serving. Cut each quesadilla into 8 wedges.

Keep it fun, keep it no-fuss! Assemble the quesadillas, then cover and refrigerate them up to 1 hour ahead of time.

High Altitude (3500–6500 ft): In step 2, bake 12 to 14 minutes.

1 Serving: Calories 70 (Calories from Fat 25); Total Fat 2.5g (Saturated Fat 1g; Trans Fat 0g); Cholesterol 5mg; Sodium 140mg; Total Carbohydrate 7g (Dietary Fiber 0g; Sugars 1g); Protein 3g % Daily Value: Vitamin A 0%; Vitamin C 0%; Calcium 4%; Iron 4% Exchanges: $^1/_2$ Starch, $^1/_2$ Fat Carbohydrate Choices: $^1/_2$

bugs in a blanket

| Prep Time: **30 minutes** | Start to Finish: **45 minutes** | 24 snacks |

1 can (11 oz) refrigerated original breadsticks

24 cocktail-size smoked link sausages (from 14-oz package)

³/₄ cup shoestring potatoes (from 1 ³/₄-oz can)

Ketchup, barbecue sauce or mustard

1 Heat oven to 375°F. Unroll dough; separate at perforations into 12 breadsticks. With knife or kitchen scissors, cut each breadstick in half crosswise, making 24 pieces.

2 Wrap each piece of dough around center of each sausage, pinching to seal and leaving each end of sausage showing. Place seam side down and ¹/₂ inch apart on ungreased large cookie sheet.

3 Bake 11 to 14 minutes or until golden brown. Immediately remove from cookie sheet; place on serving plate or tray. Cool 2 minutes.

4 Insert shoestring potatoes into baked dough to resemble legs and antennae. Decorate "bugs" with dots or stripes of ketchup.

For no-mess, no-hassle decorating, spoon the ketchup, barbecue sauce and mustard into separate small resealable food-storage plastic bags. Seal and cut a tiny hole in one bottom corner of each bag; squeeze to decorate the "bugs."

High Altitude (3500–6500 ft): No change.

1 Snack: Calories 90 (Calories from Fat 50); Total Fat 5g (Saturated Fat 2g; Trans Fat 0g); Cholesterol 10mg; Sodium 250mg; Total Carbohydrate 7g (Dietary Fiber 0g; Sugars 1g); Protein 3g % Daily Value: Vitamin A 0%; Vitamin C 0%; Calcium 0%; Iron 2% Exchanges: ¹/₂ Starch, 1 Fat Carbohydrate Choices: ¹/₂

a family
thanksgiving

Easy Caramel-Pecan Bars • Lemon-Ginger Thumbprints • Crumbleberry Pear Pie • Honeyed Pumpkin Pie with Broiled Praline Topping • Paradise Pumpkin Pie • Banana Cream Pudding Pie • Delicious Apple Cream Pie • Easy Caramel Apple Tart • Mystery Pecan Pie • Cranberry-Topped Cake • Apple-Cranberry Upside-Down Cake • Pumpkin Gingerbread with Caramel Sauce • Sour Cream Apple Squares • Streusel Pecan Pie Squares • Pumpkin Cheesecake with Praline Sauce • Pumpkin-Maple Coffee Cake • Pumpkin-Pecan Braid • Lazy Maple Crescent Pull-Aparts • Raspberry Cream Cheese Coffee Cake • Pumpkin-Rum Pistachio Loaf • White Chocolate–Iced Blueberry Loaf • Walnut, Hazelnut and Golden Raisin Wheat Rolls • Cornmeal Sage Scones • Mini Focaccia Rounds • Baked Brie and Brandied Mushrooms • Flaky Sausage Foldovers • Basil and Havarti Cheese Pinwheels • Bacon-Cheddar Pinwheels • Focaccia Dipping Sticks

easy caramel-pecan bars

extra easy

Prep Time: **25 minutes** Start to Finish: **2 hours 15 minutes** 36 bars

---

1 roll (16.5 oz) refrigerated
sugar cookies

$^3/_4$ cup caramel topping

2 tablespoons all-purpose flour

1 cup pecan pieces

1 cup flaked coconut

1 bag (6 oz) semisweet
chocolate chips (1 cup)

1 Heat oven to 350°F. Spray 13 × 9-inch pan with cooking spray. Cut cookie dough into $^1/_2$-inch slices. Arrange slices in bottom of pan. With floured fingers, press dough evenly to form crust.

2 Bake 10 to 15 minutes or until light golden brown.

3 Meanwhile, in glass measuring cup, stir caramel topping and flour until smooth.

4 Sprinkle partially baked crust with pecans, coconut and chocolate chips. Drizzle with caramel mixture.

5 Bake 15 to 20 minutes longer or until topping is bubbly. Cool completely, about 1 $^1/_2$ hours. For bars, cut into 6 rows by 6 rows.

Fat-free caramel topping will work just fine in this recipe if that's all you have on hand.

High Altitude (3500–6500 ft): In step 2, bake 12 to 17 minutes.

1 Bar: Calories 130 (Calories from Fat 60); Total Fat 7g (Saturated Fat 2.5g; Trans Fat 0.5g); Cholesterol 0mg; Sodium 65mg; Total Carbohydrate 17g (Dietary Fiber 0g; Sugars 11g); Protein 1g % Daily Value: Vitamin A 0%; Vitamin C 0%; Calcium 0%; Iron 4% Exchanges: 1 Other Carbohydrate, 1 $^1/_2$ Fat Carbohydrate Choices: 1

lemon-ginger thumbprints

extra
easy

Prep Time: **45 minutes**	Start to Finish: **45 minutes**	3 dozen cookies

1 roll (16.5 oz) refrigerated
  gingerbread cookies

3 tablespoons graham cracker
  crumbs

$^1/_2$ cup lemon curd or lemon
  pie filling

1 Heat oven to 350°F. Cut cookie dough into 3 equal pieces. Work with 1 piece of dough at a time; refrigerate remaining dough until ready to use.

2 In shallow dish, place graham cracker crumbs. Shape each piece of dough into twelve 1-inch balls; roll in crumbs to coat. Place 1 inch apart on ungreased large cookie sheet.

3 Bake 8 to 11 minutes or until cookies are almost set. Cool 2 minutes on cookie sheet. With thumb or handle of wooden spoon, make slight indentation in center of each cookie. Remove cookies from cookie sheet. Cool completely, about 15 minutes.

4 In small resealable food-storage plastic bag, place lemon curd; partially seal bag. Cut small hole in one bottom corner of bag. Squeeze bag to pipe small dollop of lemon curd into indentation in each cookie. Store in refrigerator.

Lemon curd is a rich, thick spread made of a cooked mixture of butter, sugar, egg yolks and lemon juice. Look for it in the grocery store with the jams and jellies.

High Altitude (3500–6500 ft):
No change.

1 Cookie: Calories 80 (Calories from Fat 30); Total Fat 3.5g (Saturated Fat 0.5g; Trans Fat 1g); Cholesterol 10mg; Sodium 50mg; Total Carbohydrate 11g (Dietary Fiber 0g; Sugars 7g); Protein 0g % Daily Value: Vitamin A 0%; Vitamin C 0%; Calcium 0%; Iron 0% Exchanges: $^1/_2$ Other Carbohydrate, 1 Fat Carbohydrate Choices: 1

crumbleberry pear pie

Prep Time: **20 minutes**   Start to Finish: **2 hours 25 minutes**   12 servings

CRUST

1 refrigerated pie crust
    (from 15-oz box), softened
    as directed on box

FILLING

$^1/_2$ cup butter or margarine,
    softened

$^1/_2$ cup granulated sugar

2 eggs

1 cup finely ground almonds

$^1/_4$ cup all-purpose flour

1 large firm pear or apple,
    peeled, thinly sliced

1 cup fresh or frozen raspberries
    and/or blueberries, thawed

TOPPING

$^3/_4$ cup all-purpose flour

$^1/_3$ cup packed brown sugar

$^1/_2$ teaspoon almond extract

$^1/_3$ cup butter or margarine

1 Heat oven to 350°F. Place pie crust in 9-inch glass pie plate as directed on box for One-Crust Filled Pie.

2 In large bowl, beat $^1/_2$ cup butter and the granulated sugar until light and fluffy. Beat in 1 egg at a time until well blended. Stir in almonds and $^1/_4$ cup flour just until evenly moistened. Spread mixture in crust-lined pan. Arrange pear slices on top of filling, overlapping slightly.

3 Bake 20 to 30 minutes or until filling and pears are light golden brown.

4 Meanwhile, in medium bowl, mix $^3/_4$ cup flour, the brown sugar and almond extract. Using pastry blender or fork, cut in $^1/_3$ cup butter until mixture resembles coarse crumbs.

5 Sprinkle raspberries over pear; sprinkle with topping. Bake 18 to 28 minutes or until topping is golden brown. Cool 1 hour. Serve warm. Store in refrigerator.

Grind the almonds in a food processor or in batches in a blender. Use short on/off bursts to grind them evenly, stirring once or twice. If you grind them too much, the mixture will form a paste.

High Altitude (3500–6500 ft):
No change.

1 Serving: Calories 370 (Calories from Fat 200); Total Fat 23g (Saturated Fat 10g; Trans Fat 1g); Cholesterol 70mg; Sodium 180mg; Total Carbohydrate 37g (Dietary Fiber 2g; Sugars 17g); Protein 4g % Daily Value: Vitamin A 10%; Vitamin C 2%; Calcium 4%; Iron 6% Exchanges: 1 Starch, 1 $^1/_2$ Other Carbohydrate, 4 $^1/_2$ Fat Carbohydrate Choices: 2 $^1/_2$

honeyed pumpkin pie with broiled praline topping

Prep Time: **20 minutes**   Start to Finish: **3 hours 35 minutes**   10 servings

CRUST

1 refrigerated pie crust
   (from 15-oz box), softened
   as directed on box

FILLING

1 can (15 oz) pumpkin (not
   pumpkin pie mix)

1 cup honey

$^3/_4$ teaspoon salt

$^3/_4$ teaspoon ground nutmeg

$^1/_4$ teaspoon ground allspice

4 eggs

$^3/_4$ cup evaporated milk

TOPPING

$^1/_3$ cup chopped pecans

$^1/_4$ cup packed brown sugar

2 tablespoons butter or
   margarine, melted

1 Heat oven to 375°F. Place pie crust in 10-inch deep dish pie pan as directed on box for One-Crust Filled Pie—except roll crust into 13-inch round before placing in pan.

2 In large bowl, mix pumpkin, honey, salt, nutmeg and allspice. Add eggs; blend well. Gradually add milk, beating with electric mixer on low speed until well blended. Pour into crust-lined pan.

3 Bake 45 to 55 minutes or until edge is set. Cool completely on cooling rack.

4 In small bowl, mix all topping ingredients; sprinkle over top of cooled pie. Set oven control to broil. Broil 4 to 6 inches from heat 2 to 3 minutes or until topping is bubbly. Store in refrigerator.

Pie crust dough doesn't like to be stretched to fit the pie pan, because it shrinks when baked. Instead, firmly press the dough against the side and bottom of pan without stretching it. Honey makes this pie filling softer and silkier than pumpkin pie made with sugar.

High Altitude (3500–6500 ft): Bake 50 to 60 minutes, covering edge of crust with foil during last 30 minutes of baking to prevent overbrowning.

1 Serving: Calories 340 (Calories from Fat 120); Total Fat 14g (Saturated Fat 5g; Trans Fat 0g); Cholesterol 95mg; Sodium 330mg; Total Carbohydrate 50g (Dietary Fiber 2g; Sugars 37g); Protein 5g % Daily Value: Vitamin A 140%; Vitamin C 0%; Calcium 8%; Iron 6% Exchanges: 1 Starch, 2 $^1/_2$ Other Carbohydrate, 2 $^1/_2$ Fat Carbohydrate Choices: 3

paradise pumpkin pie

Prep Time: 15 minutes   Start to Finish: 2 hours 30 minutes   8 servings

CRUST

1 refrigerated pie crust
   (from 15-oz box), softened
   as directed on box

FILLING

2 eggs, slightly beaten

$1/2$ cup sugar

1 teaspoon ground cinnamon

$1/4$ teaspoon ground ginger

$1/4$ teaspoon ground nutmeg

Dash salt

$1\,1/4$ cups (from 15-oz can)
   pumpkin (not pumpkin pie mix)

1 cup evaporated milk, whipping
   cream or half-and-half

1 package (8 oz) cream cheese

$1/4$ cup sugar

$1/2$ teaspoon vanilla

1 egg

Maple-flavored syrup, if desired

TOPPING

Sweetened whipped cream,
   if desired

1 Heat oven to 350°F. While crust is softening, in large bowl, beat 2 eggs, $1/2$ cup sugar, the cinnamon, ginger, nutmeg, salt, pumpkin and milk with wire whisk until well blended; set aside.

2 In small bowl, beat cream cheese, $1/4$ cup sugar and the vanilla with electric mixer on low speed until well blended. Add 1 egg; beat until well blended.

3 Place pie crust in 9-inch glass pie plate as directed on box for One-Crust Filled Pie. Spread cream cheese mixture on bottom of crust.

4 Carefully spoon or pour pumpkin mixture over cream cheese mixture. Cover edge of pie crust with strip of foil to prevent excessive browning. Bake 1 hour 5 minutes to 1 hour 15 minutes or until knife inserted in center comes out clean. Cool 5 minutes; brush with syrup. Cool completely, about 1 hour. Serve with sweetened whipped cream. Store in refrigerator.

A creamy cheesecake layer and a spiced pumpkin pie layer—it doesn't get much better than this!

High Altitude (3500–6500 ft):
No change.

1 Serving: Calories 380 (Calories from Fat 180); Total Fat 20g (Saturated Fat 10g, Trans Fat 0g); Cholesterol 120mg; Sodium 270mg; Total Carbohydrate 41g (Dietary Fiber 1g, Sugars 26g); Protein 7g % Daily Value: Vitamin A 130%; Vitamin C 0%; Calcium 15%; Iron 8% Exchanges: 1 Starch, 2 Other Carbohydrate, $1/2$ High-Fat Meat, 3 Fat Carbohydrate Choices: 3

pretty as pie garnishing

Adding a special touch to a slice of pie turns ordinary to extraordinary! Refrigerated pie crust makes it so easy—it's a cinch!

Add sparkle to two-crust pie by brushing top crust with water, milk or beaten egg and sprinkle with granulated sugar, colored sugar or decorator sugar before baking.

Jazz it up with pretty leaves! Using cookie cutters, cut leaf shapes from extra pie crust; sprinkle with cinnamon and sugar. Place flat on cookie sheet or drape over crumpled foil to create curved leaves. Bake at 425°F just until golden brown.

Top each slice with dollop of whipped cream or scoop of ice cream; drizzle with maple syrup and toasted pecans.

Spread top of pie with whipped cream and sprinkle with toffee bits or peanut brittle.

banana cream pudding pie

Prep Time: **30 minutes**   Start to Finish: **3 hours 40 minutes**   8 servings

CRUST

1 refrigerated pie crust
   (from 15-oz box), softened
   as directed on box

FILLING

$3/4$ cup sugar

$1/4$ cup cornstarch

$1/4$ teaspoon salt

3 cups milk

3 egg yolks, slightly beaten

2 tablespoons butter or
   margarine

2 teaspoons vanilla

2 to 3 medium bananas, sliced

TOPPING

Sweetened whipped cream or
   whipped topping, if desired

1 Heat oven to 450°F. Make pie crust as directed on box for One-Crust Baked Shell using 9-inch glass pie plate. Bake 9 to 11 minutes or until lightly browned. Cool completely, about 30 minutes.

2 Meanwhile, in 2-quart saucepan, mix sugar, cornstarch and salt. Stir in milk until smooth. Cook over medium heat, stirring constantly, until mixture boils and thickens; boil and stir 2 minutes. Remove from heat.

3 Stir about $1/4$ cup hot mixture into egg yolks. Gradually stir yolk mixture into hot mixture. Cook over medium heat, stirring constantly, just until mixture begins to bubble and is thickened. Remove from heat; stir in butter and vanilla. Cool until lukewarm, about 20 minutes.

4 Arrange banana slices in cooled baked shell. Pour cooled pudding over bananas. Refrigerate until set, at least 3 hours. Top with whipped cream. Store in refrigerator.

Add a little pizzazz by serving this pie with rum-flavored whipped cream! In chilled medium bowl, beat 1 cup whipping cream, 3 tablespoons powdered sugar and $1/2$ teaspoon rum extract with electric mixer on high speed until soft peaks form.

High Altitude (3500–6500 ft): In step 2, cook mixture over medium-high heat. In step 3, cook mixture over medium-high heat 2 minutes.

1 Serving: Calories 330 (Calories from Fat 120); Total Fat 13g (Saturated Fat 6g; Trans Fat 0g); Cholesterol 95mg; Sodium 250mg; Total Carbohydrate 47g (Dietary Fiber 0g; Sugars 27g); Protein 4g % Daily Value: Vitamin A 8%; Vitamin C 2%; Calcium 10%; Iron 0% Exchanges: 1 $1/2$ Starch, $1/2$ Fruit, 1 Other Carbohydrate, 2 $1/2$ Fat Carbohydrate Choices: 3

delicious apple cream pie

Prep Time: **35 minutes**   Start to Finish: **2 hours 25 minutes**   8 servings

CRUST

1 box (15 oz) refrigerated pie
  crusts, softened as directed
  on box

FILLING

³/₄ cup granulated sugar

3 tablespoons all-purpose flour

1 teaspoon ground cinnamon

6 cups thinly sliced peeled
  apples (6 medium)

¹/₂ cup whipping cream

1 teaspoon vanilla

TOPPING

1 egg white, beaten

1 tablespoon coarse white
  sparkling sugar or
  granulated sugar

1 Heat oven to 400°F. Make pie crusts as directed on box for Two-Crust Pie using 9-inch glass pie plate.

2 In large bowl, mix granulated sugar, flour and cinnamon; gently stir in apples. In small bowl, mix whipping cream and vanilla. Pour over apple mixture; stir gently to mix well. Spoon into crust-lined pan.

3 Top with second pie crust; seal edge and flute. Cut slits or shapes in several places in top crust. Brush top with egg white; sprinkle with coarse sugar. Cover edge of pastry with 2- to 3-inch strip of foil to prevent excessive browning; remove foil for last 15 minutes of baking.

4 Bake 40 to 50 minutes or until apples are tender and crust is golden brown. Cool completely, about 1 hour.

Look for coarse white sparkling sugar near the colored sugar in the baking aisle of large supermarkets or in kitchen specialty shops.

High Altitude (3500–6500 ft):
No change.

1 Serving: Calories 410 (Calories from Fat 170); Total Fat 19g (Saturated Fat 8g; Trans Fat 0g); Cholesterol 25mg; Sodium 230mg; Total Carbohydrate 60g (Dietary Fiber 1g; Sugars 29g); Protein 1g % Daily Value: Vitamin A 4%; Vitamin C 2%; Calcium 0%; Iron 0% Exchanges: 1 Starch, ¹/₂ Fruit, 2 ¹/₂ Other Carbohydrate, 3 ¹/₂ Fat Carbohydrate Choices: 4

Creamy, yummy and sweet describes this super-easy pie. Banana- or vanilla-flavored yogurt would taste great if you can't find the caramel flavor.

easy caramel apple tart

Prep Time: **20 minutes**   Start to Finish: **1 hour 15 minutes**   16 servings

1 box (15 oz) refrigerated pie
   crusts, softened as directed
   on box

2 containers (6 oz each) crème
   caramel thick and creamy
   low-fat yogurt

1 package (3 oz) cream cheese,
   softened

1 can (21 oz) apple pie filling
   with more fruit

3 tablespoons caramel topping

1 Heat oven to 375°F. Remove crusts from pouches; unroll 1 crust in center of ungreased large cookie sheet. Place second crust flat over first crust, matching edges and pressing to seal. With rolling pin, roll out into 14-inch round.

2 Fold $1/2$ inch of crust edge under, forming border; press to seal seam. If desired, flute edge. Prick crust generously with fork.

3 Bake 20 to 25 minutes or until golden brown. Cool completely, about 30 minutes.

4 In medium bowl, beat yogurt and cream cheese with electric mixer on medium speed until blended. Spread evenly over cooled baked crust. Spread pie filling evenly over yogurt mixture. Drizzle caramel topping over top. Cut into wedges. Store in refrigerator.

High Altitude (3500–6500 ft):
Bake 17 to 22 minutes.

1 Serving: Calories 200 (Calories from Fat 80); Total Fat 9g (Saturated Fat 4g; Trans Fat 0g); Cholesterol 10mg; Sodium 150mg; Total Carbohydrate 27g (Dietary Fiber 0g; Sugars 12g); Protein 2g % Daily Value: Vitamin A 4%; Vitamin C 0%; Calcium 4%; Iron 0% Exchanges: 1 Starch, 1 Other Carbohydrate, 1 $1/2$ Fat Carbohydrate Choices: 2

mystery pecan pie

Prep Time: **15 minutes**	Start to Finish: **3 hours**	8 servings

CRUST

1 refrigerated pie crust
(from 15-oz box), softened
as directed on box

CREAM CHEESE LAYER

1 package (8 oz) cream cheese,
softened

$1/3$ cup sugar

$1/4$ teaspoon salt

1 teaspoon vanilla

1 egg

PECAN LAYER

3 eggs

$1/4$ cup sugar

1 cup corn syrup

1 teaspoon vanilla

$1 1/4$ cups chopped pecans

1 Heat oven to 375°F. Place pie crust in 9-inch glass pie plate as directed on box for One-Crust Filled Pie.

2 In small bowl, beat all cream cheese layer ingredients with electric mixer on low speed until well blended and smooth. Set aside.

3 In another small bowl, beat 3 eggs with electric mixer on medium speed. Add remaining pecan layer ingredients except pecans; beat until well blended.

4 Spread cream cheese mixture in bottom of crust-lined pan. Sprinkle with pecans. Gently pour egg mixture over pecans. Cover crust edge with 2- to 3-inch-wide strips of foil to prevent excessive browning; remove foil during last 15 minutes of baking.

5 Bake 35 to 45 minutes or until center is set. Cool completely, about 2 hours, before serving. Store in refrigerator.

There is no mystery to why this pie is a most-requested recipe—the surprise cream cheese layer makes it taste heavenly! Try using cashews or even coarsely chopped macadamia nuts instead of the pecans for a flavor twist.

High Altitude (3500–6500 ft):
Bake 40 to 50 minutes.

1 Serving: Calories 570 (Calories from Fat 290); Total Fat 32g (Saturated Fat 11g; Trans Fat 0g); Cholesterol 140mg; Sodium 350mg; Total Carbohydrate 64g (Dietary Fiber 2g; Sugars 32g); Protein 7g % Daily Value: Vitamin A 10%; Vitamin C 0%; Calcium 4%; Iron 6% Exchanges: 2 Starch, 2 $1/2$ Other Carbohydrate, 6 Fat Carbohydrate Choices: 4

cranberry-topped cake

Prep Time: **30 minutes**   Start to Finish: **1 hour 50 minutes**   9 servings

TOPPING

$2/3$ cup canned jellied cranberry
   sauce (from 16-oz can)

$1/3$ cup chopped walnuts or
   pecans

3 tablespoons sugar

1 teaspoon grated lemon peel

$1/4$ teaspoon ground cinnamon,
   if desired

CAKE

2 cups all-purpose flour

2 teaspoons baking powder

$1/2$ to 1 teaspoon salt

1 cup sugar

$1/3$ cup butter or margarine,
   softened

1 teaspoon lemon extract or
   grated lemon peel

2 eggs

$3/4$ cup milk

1 Heat oven to 350°F. Generously grease 9-inch square pan with shortening; lightly flour. In medium bowl, mix all topping ingredients. Set aside.

2 In small bowl, mix flour, baking powder and salt. In large bowl, beat 1 cup sugar and the butter with electric mixer on medium speed until well blended. Add lemon extract and eggs; beat well. Alternately add flour mixture and milk to butter mixture, beating until well combined. Pour batter into pan.

3 Drop topping by teaspoonfuls evenly onto batter. Spread topping over batter.

4 Bake 42 to 47 minutes or until toothpick inserted in center comes out clean. Cool at least 30 minutes. Serve warm or cool.

Do you have leftover jellied cranberry sauce from your turkey day dinner? Perfect! Use it for this tasty little cake. Serve with vanilla ice cream or frozen yogurt.

High Altitude (3500–6500 ft): Reduce baking powder to 1 $1/2$ teaspoons. Bake 47 to 52 minutes.

1 Serving: Calories 370 (Calories from Fat 110); Total Fat 12g (Saturated Fat 3g; Trans Fat 1.5g); Cholesterol 50mg; Sodium 270mg; Total Carbohydrate 58g (Dietary Fiber 1g; Sugars 35g); Protein 6g % Daily Value: Vitamin A 2%; Vitamin C 0%; Calcium 10%; Iron 10% Exchanges: 2 Starch, 2 Other Carbohydrate, 2 Fat Carbohydrate Choices: 4

apple-cranberry upside-down cake

Prep Time: **15 minutes**   Start to Finish: **1 hour 20 minutes**   *12 servings*

TOPPING

¹/₂ cup packed brown sugar

¹/₄ cup butter or margarine, melted

1 large apple, peeled, sliced

¹/₄ cup sweetened dried cranberries

CAKE

1 box (15.6 oz) cranberry quick bread and muffin mix

³/₄ cup water

2 tablespoons vegetable oil

2 eggs

1 Heat oven to 350°F. Grease 10-inch ovenproof skillet or 10-inch deep dish pie pan with shortening. In small bowl, mix brown sugar and butter. Spread in skillet. Arrange apple slices and cranberries over brown sugar mixture.

2 In large bowl, stir all cake ingredients 50 to 75 strokes with spoon until mix is moistened. Spoon batter over fruit.

3 Bake 35 to 40 minutes or until toothpick inserted in center comes out clean (if cast-iron or dark-colored skillet is used, start checking for doneness after 30 minutes). Cool in pan 2 minutes. Invert cake onto serving plate. Cool 20 minutes. Serve warm or cool.

If you love the flavor—but not the price—of dried cherries, look for cherry-flavored dried cranberries and use those instead of regular dried cranberries.

High Altitude (3500–6500 ft): Add 1 tablespoon all-purpose flour to dry quick bread & muffin mix.

1 Serving: Calories 270 (Calories from Fat 90); Total Fat 10g (Saturated Fat 3.5g; Trans Fat 0.5g); Cholesterol 45mg; Sodium 210mg; Total Carbohydrate 42g (Dietary Fiber 0g; Sugars 28g); Protein 3g % Daily Value: Vitamin A 4%; Vitamin C 0%; Calcium 0%; Iron 4% Exchanges: 1 Starch, 2 Other Carbohydrate, 1 ¹/₂ Fat Carbohydrate Choices: 3

pumpkin gingerbread with caramel sauce

Prep Time: **20 minutes**   Start to Finish: **1 hour 10 minutes**   12 servings

GINGERBREAD

2 ¹/₄ cups all-purpose flour

¹/₂ cup granulated sugar

²/₃ cup butter or margarine

³/₄ cup coarsely chopped pecans

1 ¹/₂ teaspoons ground ginger

1 teaspoon baking soda

¹/₂ teaspoon ground cinnamon

¹/₄ teaspoon salt

¹/₄ teaspoon ground cloves

³/₄ cup buttermilk*

¹/₂ cup light molasses

¹/₂ cup canned pumpkin (not pumpkin pie mix)

1 egg

SAUCE

¹/₂ cup butter or margarine

1 ¹/₄ cups packed brown sugar

2 tablespoons light corn syrup

¹/₂ cup whipping cream

TOPPING

Ice cream, if desired

Chopped pecans, if desired

1 Heat oven to 350°F. In large bowl, mix flour and granulated sugar. With pastry blender or fork, cut in ²/₃ cup butter until mixture resembles fine crumbs. Stir in pecans. Press 1 ¹/₄ cups crumb mixture in bottom of ungreased 9-inch square pan.

2 To remaining crumb mixture, add all remaining gingerbread ingredients; mix well. Pour evenly over crumb crust in pan.

3 Bake 40 to 50 minutes or until toothpick inserted in center comes out clean.

4 In medium saucepan, melt ¹/₂ cup butter. Stir in brown sugar and corn syrup. Heat to boiling. Cook about 1 minute, stirring constantly, until sugar dissolves. Stir in whipping cream; return to boiling. Remove from heat. Serve warm sauce over warm gingerbread. Top with ice cream; sprinkle with chopped pecans.

* To substitute for buttermilk, use 2 ¹/₄ teaspoons vinegar or lemon juice plus milk to make ³/₄ cup.

Get a head start on holiday gift giving with this extra-special buttery-crusted gingerbread and luscious caramel sauce, perfect for those gingerbread lovers on your list. Bake it in a decorative disposable pan with a lid, and pour the sauce into a pretty glass jar.

High Altitude (3500–6500 ft): Add 3 tablespoons all-purpose flour to remaining crumb mixture.

1 Serving: Calories 520 (Calories from Fat 240); Total Fat 27g (Saturated Fat 14g; Trans Fat 1g); Cholesterol 75mg; Sodium 320mg; Total Carbohydrate 65g (Dietary Fiber 2g; Sugars 41g); Protein 5g % Daily Value: Vitamin A 45%; Vitamin C 0%; Calcium 10%; Iron 15% Exchanges: 1 Starch, 3 ¹/₂ Other Carbohydrate, 5 Fat Carbohydrate Choices: 4

sour cream apple squares

| Prep Time: **15 minutes** | Start to Finish: **50 minutes** | 12 to 15 squares |

2 cups all-purpose flour

2 cups packed brown sugar

$1/2$ cup butter or margarine,
  softened

1 cup chopped nuts

1 to 2 teaspoons ground
  cinnamon

1 teaspoon baking soda

$1/2$ teaspoon salt

1 cup sour cream

1 teaspoon vanilla

1 egg

2 cups finely chopped peeled
  apples (2 medium)

Sweetened whipped cream,
  if desired

1 Heat oven to 350°F. In large bowl, beat flour, brown sugar and butter with electric mixer on low speed until crumbly. Stir in nuts. In ungreased 13 × 9-inch pan, press 2 $3/4$ cups crumb mixture.

2 Add cinnamon, baking soda, salt, sour cream, vanilla and egg to remaining crumb mixture; blend well. Stir in apples. Spoon evenly over crumb crust in pan.

3 Bake 25 to 35 minutes or until toothpick inserted in center comes out clean. Serve with whipped cream.

To make Sour Cream Pear Squares, use your favorite ripe variety of pears instead of the apples. Make spiced sweetened whipped cream by adding $1/2$ teaspoon ground cinnamon, ginger, nutmeg or pumpkin pie spice to the whipped cream.

High Altitude (3500–6500 ft):
Heat oven to 375°F.

1 Square: Calories 410 (Calories from Fat 170); Total Fat 18g (Saturated Fat 8g; Trans Fat 0.5g); Cholesterol 50mg; Sodium 290mg; Total Carbohydrate 57g (Dietary Fiber 2g; Sugars 38g); Protein 5g % Daily Value: Vitamin A 8%; Vitamin C 0%; Calcium 8%; Iron 10% Exchanges: 1 Starch, 3 Other Carbohydrate, 3 $1/2$ Fat Carbohydrate Choices: 4

streusel pecan pie squares

| Prep Time: **15 minutes** | Start to Finish: **1 hour** | 15 servings |

CRUST

3 cups all-purpose flour

³/₄ cup packed brown sugar

1 ¹/₂ cups cold butter or
    margarine

FILLING

³/₄ cup packed brown sugar

1 ¹/₂ cups corn syrup or maple-
    flavored syrup

1 cup milk

¹/₃ cup butter or margarine,
    melted

1 teaspoon vanilla

4 eggs

1 ¹/₂ cups chopped pecans

TOPPING

Whipped cream or ice cream,
    if desired

1 Heat oven to 400°F. In large bowl, mix all crust ingredients until crumbly. Reserve 2 cups crumbs for filling and topping. Press remaining crumbs in bottom and ³/₄ inch up sides of ungreased 15 × 10 × 1-inch pan. Bake 10 minutes.

2 In large bowl, mix ¹/₄ cup of the reserved crumbs and all filling ingredients except pecans. Stir in pecans. Pour over partially baked crust; bake 10 minutes.

3 Reduce oven temperature to 350°F. Sprinkle remaining 1 ³/₄ cups reserved crumbs over filling; bake 20 to 25 minutes longer or until filling is set and crumbs are golden brown. Serve with whipped cream.

Expect rave reviews for these sensational buttery pecan pie squares! If you're a fan of real maple syrup, by all means, go ahead and use that instead of the corn syrup or maple-flavored syrup.

High Altitude (3500–6500 ft):
No change.

1 Serving: Calories 590 (Calories from Fat 290); Total Fat 32g (Saturated Fat 16g; Trans Fat 1.5g); Cholesterol 115mg; Sodium 230mg; Total Carbohydrate 69g (Dietary Fiber 2g; Sugars 35g); Protein 6g % Daily Value: Vitamin A 15%; Vitamin C 0%; Calcium 6%; Iron 10% Exchanges: 2 Starch, 2 ¹/₂ Other Carbohydrate, 6 Fat Carbohydrate Choices: 4 ¹/₂

pumpkin cheesecake with praline sauce

| Prep Time: **30 minutes** | Start to Finish: **7 hours 30 minutes** | 16 servings |

CRUST

1 tablespoon butter, softened

1 ¼ cups finely chopped pecans

¼ cup unseasoned dry bread crumbs

2 tablespoons granulated sugar

2 tablespoons butter, melted

FILLING

4 packages (8 oz each) cream cheese, softened

1 cup packed brown sugar

²/₃ cup granulated sugar

5 eggs

¼ cup all-purpose flour

2 teaspoons pumpkin pie spice

1 can (15 oz) pumpkin (not pumpkin pie mix)

2 tablespoons brandy, if desired

SAUCE

½ cup packed brown sugar

¼ cup water

¼ cup butter

1 egg, beaten

¼ cup chopped pecans

½ teaspoon vanilla

1 Heat oven to 350°F. Grease 9-inch springform pan with 1 tablespoon butter. In medium bowl, mix 1 ¼ cups pecans, the bread crumbs and 2 tablespoons granulated sugar. Drizzle melted butter over pecan mixture; toss to combine. Press into bottom and up side of pan; refrigerate.

2 In large bowl, beat cream cheese until fluffy. Gradually beat in 1 cup brown sugar and ²/₃ cup granulated sugar until smooth. Beat in 5 eggs, 1 at a time, until well blended. In small bowl, mix flour, pumpkin pie spice, pumpkin and brandy. Gradually add to cream cheese mixture; beat until smooth. Pour into crust.

3 Bake 1 hour 20 minutes to 1 hour 30 minutes or until center is set. Turn oven off; let cheesecake stand in oven with door open at least 8 inches for 30 minutes. Remove from oven; cool to room temperature on cooling rack. Remove side of pan. Refrigerate overnight.

4 In small saucepan, heat ½ cup brown sugar, the water and ¼ cup butter to boiling over medium heat; boil 2 minutes. Gradually blend small amount of hot syrup into beaten egg. Return egg mixture to saucepan; cook over low heat 1 minute, stirring constantly. Remove from heat; stir in ¼ cup pecans and the vanilla. Serve sauce slightly warm over each wedge of cheesecake.

High Altitude (3500–6500 ft): Place pan of water on bottom oven rack. Heat oven to 325°F. Use 10-inch springform pan. In step 3, increase bake time 5 minutes.

1 Serving: Calories 500 (Calories from Fat 310); Total Fat 34g (Saturated Fat 17g; Trans Fat 1g); Cholesterol 155mg; Sodium 250mg; Total Carbohydrate 38g (Dietary Fiber 2g; Sugars 32g); Protein 8g % Daily Value: Vitamin A 100%; Vitamin C 0%; Calcium 10%; Iron 10% Exchanges: ½ Starch, 2 Other Carbohydrate, 1 High-Fat Meat, 5 Fat Carbohydrate Choices: 2 ½

pumpkin-maple coffee cake

Prep Time: **30 minutes**   Start to Finish: **1 hour 20 minutes**   9 servings

COFFEE CAKE

1 $^1/_2$ cups all-purpose flour

$^3/_4$ cup packed brown sugar

2 teaspoons baking powder

$^1/_2$ teaspoon salt

$^1/_4$ teaspoon baking soda

$^2/_3$ cup buttermilk*

$^1/_2$ cup canned pumpkin (not
pumpkin pie mix)

$^1/_3$ cup vegetable oil

$^1/_2$ teaspoon imitation maple
flavor

2 eggs, beaten

TOPPING

$^1/_2$ cup granulated sugar

1 teaspoon ground cinnamon

1 teaspoon imitation maple
flavor

1 Heat oven to 350°F. Spray bottom only of 9-inch square pan with cooking spray. In large bowl, mix all coffee cake ingredients until dry ingredients are moistened.

2 In small bowl, mix granulated sugar and cinnamon. Add 1 teaspoon maple flavor; mix well with fork.

3 Spread half of batter in pan. Sprinkle with half of topping. Spoon remaining batter over top; spread evenly. Sprinkle with remaining topping.

4 Bake 25 to 35 minutes or until toothpick inserted in center comes out clean. Cool 15 minutes. Serve warm.

* To substitute for buttermilk, use 2 teaspoons vinegar or lemon juice plus milk to make $^2/_3$ cup.

Jazz up your butter by making holiday-shaped butter pats. Cut $^1/_4$-inch slices of butter and use small canapé or cookie cutters to cut shapes out of each slice. Sprinkle with edible glitter or colored sugar, if you'd like. Cover and refrigerate until serving time.

High Altitude (3500–6500 ft):
Increase flour to 1 $^2/_3$ cups.

1 Serving: Calories 300 (Calories from Fat 90); Total Fat 10g (Saturated Fat 2g; Trans Fat 0g); Cholesterol 50mg; Sodium 310mg; Total Carbohydrate 48g (Dietary Fiber 1g; Sugars 30g); Protein 4g % Daily Value: Vitamin A 45%; Vitamin C 0%; Calcium 10%; Iron 10% Exchanges: 1 Starch, 2 Other Carbohydrate, 2 Fat Carbohydrate Choices: 3

pumpkin-pecan braid

Prep Time: **20 minutes**   Start to Finish: **50 minutes**   6 servings

COFFEE CAKE

³/₄ cup canned pumpkin
   (not pumpkin pie mix)
¹/₃ cup packed brown sugar
1 teaspoon ground cinnamon
¹/₈ teaspoon ground ginger
¹/₈ teaspoon ground nutmeg
1 egg, separated
¹/₂ cup chopped pecans
1 can (8 oz) refrigerated crescent
   dinner rolls

GLAZE

¹/₂ cup powdered sugar
2 to 3 teaspoons milk
1 tablespoon chopped pecans

1   Heat oven to 350°F. Spray cookie sheet with cooking spray. In medium bowl, mix pumpkin, brown sugar, cinnamon, ginger, nutmeg and egg yolk until well blended. Stir in ¹/₂ cup pecans.

2   Unroll dough on cookie sheet; press perforations and edges to seal. Press to form 13 × 7-inch rectangle. Spread filling in 3 ¹/₂-inch-wide strip lengthwise down center of dough rectangle to within 1 inch of ends.

3   With scissors or sharp knife, make cuts 1 inch apart on long sides of dough rectangle just to edge of filling. Fold strips at an angle across filling, overlapping ends and alternating from side to side. In small bowl, beat egg white until foamy; brush over dough.

4   Bake 20 to 30 minutes or until deep golden brown. Immediately remove from cookie sheet; place on serving platter.

5   In small bowl, blend powdered sugar and enough milk for desired drizzling consistency. Drizzle over warm coffee cake. Sprinkle with 1 tablespoon pecans.

Turn classic holiday pantry ingredients—canned pumpkin, spices and pecans—into a laid-back morning treat. The braid comes together easily with crescent roll dough, and the aroma will get your family to rise and greet the day.

High Altitude (3500–6500 ft):
No change.

1 Serving: Calories 330 (Calories from Fat 150); Total Fat 16g (Saturated Fat 3.5g; Trans Fat 2g); Cholesterol 35mg; Sodium 310mg; Total Carbohydrate 41g (Dietary Fiber 3g; Sugars 26g); Protein 5g % Daily Value: Vitamin A 100%; Vitamin C 0%; Calcium 4%; Iron 10% Exchanges: 1 Starch, 2 Other Carbohydrate, 3 Fat Carbohydrate Choices: 3

lazy maple crescent pull-aparts

Prep Time: **15 minutes**	Start to Finish: **40 minutes**	12 rolls

$^1/_4$ cup butter or margarine

$^1/_4$ cup packed brown sugar

2 tablespoons maple-flavored
  syrup

$^1/_4$ cup chopped pecans or
  walnuts

1 can (8 oz) refrigerated crescent
  dinner rolls

1 tablespoon granulated sugar

$^1/_2$ teaspoon ground cinnamon

1 Heat oven to 375°F. In ungreased 8- or 9-inch round cake pan, mix butter, brown sugar and syrup. Heat in oven 2 to 4 minutes or until butter melts; blend well. Sprinkle with pecans.

2 Remove dough from can in 2 rolled sections. DO NOT UNROLL DOUGH. Cut each roll of dough into 6 slices. In small bowl, mix granulated sugar and cinnamon; dip both sides of each slice in sugar mixture. Arrange slices over butter mixture in pan; sprinkle with any remaining sugar mixture.

3 Bake 17 to 23 minutes or until golden brown. Cool 1 minute; invert onto serving plate. Serve warm.

Arrange these rolls in a basket lined with a decorative holiday napkin. To keep the rolls warm, cover them with the four corners of the napkin or put another napkin on top.

High Altitude (3500–6500 ft):
No change.

2 Rolls: Calories 310 (Calories from Fat 170); Total Fat 19g (Saturated Fat 8g; Trans Fat 2.5g); Cholesterol 20mg; Sodium 360mg; Total Carbohydrate 32g (Dietary Fiber 0g; Sugars 16g); Protein 3g % Daily Value: Vitamin A 4%; Vitamin C 0%; Calcium 2%; Iron 6% Exchanges: 1 Starch, 1 Other Carbohydrate, 3 $^1/_2$ Fat Carbohydrate Choices: 2

raspberry cream cheese coffee cake

Prep Time: **25 minutes**   Start to Finish: **1 hour 35 minutes**   16 servings

2 ¹/₄ cups all-purpose flour

³/₄ cup sugar

³/₄ cup butter or margarine

¹/₂ teaspoon baking powder

¹/₂ teaspoon baking soda

¹/₄ teaspoon salt

³/₄ cup sour cream

1 teaspoon almond extract

1 egg

1 package (8 oz) cream cheese,
  softened

¹/₄ cup sugar

1 egg

¹/₂ cup raspberry preserves

¹/₂ cup sliced almonds

1 Heat oven to 350°F. Grease bottom and side of 9- or 10-inch springform pan with shortening; lightly flour. In large bowl, mix flour and ³/₄ cup sugar. With pastry blender or fork, cut in butter until mixture resembles coarse crumbs. Reserve 1 cup of the crumb mixture.

2 To remaining crumb mixture, add baking powder, baking soda, salt, sour cream, almond extract and 1 egg; blend well. Spread batter over bottom and 2 inches up side (about ¹/₄ inch thick) of pan.

3 In small bowl, blend cream cheese, ¹/₄ cup sugar and 1 egg. Pour into batter-lined pan. Carefully spoon preserves evenly over cream cheese mixture. In another small bowl, mix reserved crumb mixture and almonds. Sprinkle over preserves.

4 Bake 45 to 55 minutes or until cream cheese filling is set and crust is deep golden brown. Cool 15 minutes; remove side of pan. Serve warm or cool. Store in refrigerator.

This is an absolute favorite of everyone working in the test kitchens; it's very easy to make, special and delicious. It would make a lovely gift or brunch favorite—count on bringing home an empty plate!

High Altitude (3500–6500 ft): No change.

1 Serving: Calories 320 (Calories from Fat 160); Total Fat 18g (Saturated Fat 10g; Trans Fat 0.5g); Cholesterol 70mg; Sodium 210mg; Total Carbohydrate 34g (Dietary Fiber 0g; Sugars 18g); Protein 5g % Daily Value: Vitamin A 10%; Vitamin C 0%; Calcium 4%; Iron 8% Exchanges: 1 Starch, 1 ¹/₂ Other Carbohydrate, 3 ¹/₂ Fat Carbohydrate Choices: 2

pumpkin-rum pistachio loaf

Prep Time: **10 minutes**   Start to Finish: **2 hours 25 minutes**   3 loaves (8 slices each)

BREAD

$^1/_2$ cup raisins

2 tablespoons rum, or 1
  teaspoon rum extract plus
  water to make 2 tablespoons

Water

1 box (14 oz) pumpkin quick
  bread & muffin mix

3 tablespoons vegetable oil

2 eggs

$^1/_2$ cup coarsely chopped shelled
  pistachio nuts

GLAZE

$^1/_4$ cup sugar

2 tablespoons water

1 tablespoon butter

1 tablespoon rum, or $^1/_2$
  teaspoon rum extract plus
  water to make 1 tablespoon

1 In small bowl, soak raisins in 2 tablespoons rum for 30 minutes. Drain off rum into 1-cup glass measuring cup. Add enough water to make 1 cup liquid; set aside for bread batter.

2 Heat oven to 350°F. Grease bottoms only of three 5 × 3-inch foil loaf pans with shortening; lightly flour. In large bowl, stir quick bread mix, reserved 1 cup liquid, oil and eggs 50 to 75 strokes with spoon until mix is moistened. Stir in soaked raisins and pistachios. Pour batter evenly into pans. Bake 40 to 45 minutes or until toothpick inserted in center comes out clean.

3 Meanwhile, in small saucepan, heat sugar, 2 tablespoons water and the butter to boiling over medium-low heat, stirring constantly, until sugar is dissolved. Boil 3 minutes, stirring constantly. Remove from heat; stir in 1 tablespoon rum.

4 Poke surface of loaves with toothpick. Brush top of each loaf with glaze. Cool completely, about 1 hour. Wrap tightly; store in refrigerator.

How about creating Pumpkin-Rum Macadamia Loaf?
Just substitute chopped macadamia nuts for the pistachios; after glazing the loaves, sprinkle each with plain or toasted coconut for extra tropical flavor!

High Altitude (3500–6500 ft): Follow High Altitude directions on quick bread & muffin mix box.

1 Slice: Calories 130 (Calories from Fat 40); Total Fat 4.5g (Saturated Fat 1g; Trans Fat 0g); Cholesterol 20mg; Sodium 85mg; Total Carbohydrate 19g (Dietary Fiber 0g; Sugars 12g); Protein 2g % Daily Value: Vitamin A 0%; Vitamin C 0%; Calcium 0%; Iron 4% Exchanges: $^1/_2$ Starch, $^1/_2$ Other Carbohydrate, 1 Fat Carbohydrate Choices: 1

white chocolate–iced blueberry loaf

Prep Time: **10 minutes**	Start to Finish: **3 hours 10 minutes**	1 loaf (12 slices)

BREAD

2 1/2 cups all-purpose flour

1 cup granulated sugar

3 teaspoons baking powder

1/2 teaspoon salt

1/4 teaspoon ground allspice,
   if desired

1 cup buttermilk*

1/4 cup butter or margarine,
   melted

2 eggs

1 1/2 cups fresh or frozen (do not
   thaw) blueberries

1/2 cup chopped pecans

ICING

1/4 cup white vanilla baking chips

3 tablespoons powdered sugar

1 to 2 tablespoons milk

1 Heat oven to 350°F. Grease bottom only of 9 × 5-inch loaf pan with shortening. In large bowl, mix flour, granulated sugar, baking powder, salt and allspice with spoon. Beat in buttermilk, butter and eggs until blended. Stir in blueberries and pecans. Spread batter in pan.

2 Bake 1 hour 15 minutes to 1 hour 20 minutes or until toothpick inserted in center comes out clean. Cool in pan on cooling rack 10 minutes.

3 Run knife around edges of pan to loosen loaf. Remove loaf from pan; place on cooling rack. Cool completely, about 1 hour 30 minutes.

4 In small microwavable bowl, microwave baking chips on High 30 seconds. Stir until melted; if necessary, microwave in additional 10-second increments until melted. Beat in powdered sugar and enough milk until smooth and desired drizzling consistency. Drizzle icing over loaf. Let stand until icing is set before storing.

*To substitute for buttermilk, use 1 tablespoon vinegar or lemon juice plus milk to make 1 cup.

This makes a delicious gift. Insert toothpicks into the top surface of the loaf to protect the icing from sticking. Then wrap the loaf in colored plastic wrap and tie with a pretty bow.

High Altitude (3500-6500 ft): Decrease baking powder to 1 1/2 teaspoons.

1 Slice: Calories 300 (Calories from Fat 90); Total Fat 10g (Saturated Fat 4.5g; Trans Fat 0g); Cholesterol 45mg; Sodium 290mg; Total Carbohydrate 46g (Dietary Fiber 2g; Sugars 25g); Protein 6g % Daily Value: Vitamin A 4%; Vitamin C 0%; Calcium 10%; Iron 10% Exchanges: 1 1/2 Starch, 1 1/2 Other Carbohydrate, 2 Fat Carbohydrate Choices: 3

walnut, hazelnut and golden raisin wheat rolls

Prep Time: **40 minutes**   Start to Finish: **3 hours 50 minutes**   18 rolls

5 $^1/_2$ to 6 $^1/_2$ cups bread flour

1 package regular active
   dry yeast

2 $^1/_2$ cups water heated to
   100°F to 105°F

$^3/_4$ cup golden raisins

$^3/_4$ cup whole wheat flour

2 $^1/_2$ teaspoons salt

$^3/_4$ cup coarsely chopped
   walnuts, toasted*

$^3/_4$ cup coarsely chopped
   hazelnuts (filberts)

Water

1 In medium bowl, mix 2 cups of the bread flour and the yeast. Stir in 1 $^1/_2$ cups of the warm water to form a loose starter dough. Let rest 15 to 30 minutes. In small bowl, mix raisins and remaining 1 cup warm water. Let stand 15 minutes.

2 Grease cookie sheets with shortening. In large bowl, mix 3 $^1/_2$ cups of the remaining bread flour, whole wheat flour and salt.

3 Stir raisins with water into starter dough until well mixed. Add starter mixture to whole wheat flour mixture; stir until soft dough forms. Turn dough out onto floured surface; knead 10 to 12 minutes, adding $^1/_2$ to 1 cup flour until dough is smooth and elastic. Dough will be slightly sticky. Knead nuts into dough.

4 Spray large bowl with cooking spray. Place dough in bowl; cover loosely with sprayed plastic wrap and cloth towel. Let rise in warm place (80°F to 85°F) until doubled in size, about 1 $^1/_2$ hours.

5 Punch down dough several times to remove all air bubbles. Divide dough into 18 pieces. Shape each piece into a ball; place on cookie sheets. Cover; let rise until doubled in size, about 1 hour.

6 Heat oven to 425°F. Uncover dough; brush tops of rolls lightly with water. Bake 17 to 22 minutes or until golden brown.

* To toast walnuts, bake uncovered in ungreased shallow pan in 350°F oven 6 to 10 minutes, stirring occasionally, until light brown.

High Altitude (3500–6500 ft):
No change.

1 Roll: Calories 250 (Calories from Fat 60); Total Fat 7g (Saturated Fat 0.5g; Trans Fat 0g); Cholesterol 0mg; Sodium 330mg; Total Carbohydrate 42g (Dietary Fiber 3g; Sugars 4g); Protein 7g % Daily Value: Vitamin A 0%; Vitamin C 0%; Calcium 2%; Iron 15% Exchanges: 1 $^1/_2$ Starch, 1 $^1/_2$ Other Carbohydrate, 1 Fat Carbohydrate Choices: 3

cornmeal sage scones

Prep Time: **15 minutes**   Start to Finish: **45 minutes**   8 scones

1 ¼ cups all-purpose flour

½ cup yellow cornmeal

¼ cup grated Parmesan cheese

2 teaspoons baking powder

½ teaspoon baking soda

½ teaspoon salt

¾ teaspoon dried sage leaves,
   crumbled

¼ cup butter or margarine

¾ cup buttermilk*

1 Heat oven to 425°F. Spray cookie sheet with cooking spray. In large bowl, mix flour, cornmeal, cheese, baking powder, baking soda, salt and sage.

2 Using pastry blender or fork, cut in butter until mixture resembles coarse crumbs. Add buttermilk; stir just until dry ingredients are moistened.

3 On lightly floured surface, gently knead dough 10 times. Place on cookie sheet; roll or pat dough into 6 ½-inch round. Cut into 8 wedges; do not separate.

4 Bake 20 to 25 minutes or until light golden brown. Cool 5 minutes. Cut into wedges. Serve warm.

*To substitute for buttermilk, use 2 ¼ teaspoons vinegar or lemon juice plus milk to make ¾ cup.

Scones are not just for breakfast anymore—move over dinner rolls, savory scones are here! Before baking the scones, brush them with additional buttermilk and sprinkle with grated Parmesan cheese.

High Altitude (3500–6500 ft):
No change.

1 Scone: Calories 180 (Calories from Fat 70); Total Fat 7g (Saturated Fat 4.5g; Trans Fat 0g); Cholesterol 20mg; Sodium 460mg; Total Carbohydrate 23g (Dietary Fiber 0g; Sugars 1g); Protein 5g % Daily Value: Vitamin A 4%; Vitamin C 0%; Calcium 15%; Iron 8% Exchanges: 1 ½ Starch, 1 ½ Fat Carbohydrate Choices: 1 ½

mini focaccia rounds

Prep Time: **10 minutes**   Start to Finish: **25 minutes**   8 servings

1 can (11 oz) refrigerated
   original breadsticks

2 tablespoons olive or
   vegetable oil

1 tablespoon grated Parmesan
   cheese

1 teaspoon dried rosemary
   leaves, crushed

1 teaspoon dried basil leaves

1 teaspoon instant dried minced
   or chopped onion

1 Heat oven to 375°F. Lightly grease cookie sheets with shortening. Remove dough from can. Separate into 8 coils. DO NOT UNROLL BREADSTICKS. Place coils on cookie sheets. Press each coil into 4-inch round. Drizzle with oil.

2 In small bowl, mix cheese, rosemary, basil and onion; sprinkle over dough.

3 Bake 8 to 15 minutes or until golden brown.

Oh so good! These individual focaccias would taste great with any kind of soup, stew or pasta main dish. Substitute your favorite herbs if you'd like.

High Altitude (3500–6500 ft):
No change.

1 Serving: Calories 140 (Calories from Fat 50); Total Fat 6g (Saturated Fat 1g; Trans Fat 0g); Cholesterol 0mg; Sodium 290mg; Total Carbohydrate 19g (Dietary Fiber 0g; Sugars 2g); Protein 3g % Daily Value: Vitamin A 0%; Vitamin C 0%; Calcium 0%; Iron 6% Exchanges: 1 Starch, $^1/_2$ Other Carbohydrate, 1 Fat Carbohydrate Choices: 1

baked brie and brandied mushrooms

1 tablespoon butter or margarine

2 tablespoons slivered almonds

1 cup chopped fresh mushrooms

2 cloves garlic, finely chopped

1 teaspoon chopped fresh or $^1/_4$ teaspoon dried tarragon leaves

$^1/_8$ teaspoon pepper

1 tablespoon brandy

1 round (8 oz) Brie cheese

2 sprigs fresh tarragon, if desired

1 Heat oven to 375°F. In medium skillet, melt butter over medium heat. Add almonds; cook and stir 2 to 3 minutes or until almonds are browned. Stir in mushrooms, garlic, tarragon, pepper and brandy. Cook and stir 1 to 2 minutes or until mushrooms are tender. Remove from heat.

2 In ungreased decorative shallow baking dish or 8- or 9-inch glass pie plate, place cheese; spoon mushrooms over top.

3 Bake 10 to 12 minutes or until cheese is soft. Garnish with tarragon sprigs. Serve as a dip, or spread on melba toast rounds or crackers.

Brie is a soft, rich and buttery cheese with an edible white coating or rind. When heated, it becomes very soft and spreadable. Now is the time to pull out those whimsical holiday-themed spreaders you have stored away!

High Altitude (3500–6500 ft): No change.

1 Serving: Calories 60 (Calories from Fat 45); Total Fat 5g (Saturated Fat 3g; Trans Fat 0g); Cholesterol 15mg; Sodium 95mg; Total Carbohydrate 0g (Dietary Fiber 0g; Sugars 0g); Protein 3g % Daily Value: Vitamin A 2%; Vitamin C 0%; Calcium 2%; Iron 0% Exchanges: $^1/_2$ High-Fat Meat Carbohydrate Choices: 0

flaky sausage foldovers

extra easy

Prep Time: **20 minutes**	Start to Finish: **40 minutes**	22 appetizers

6 oz bulk spicy pork sausage

$^1/_4$ teaspoon garlic powder

1 can (15 oz) pizza sauce

1 box (15 oz) refrigerated pie
    crusts, softened as directed
    on box

1 egg, beaten

1 Heat oven to 425°F. In 10-inch skillet, cook sausage over medium-high heat, stirring occasionally, until thoroughly cooked; drain well. Stir in garlic powder. Add $^1/_4$ cup of the pizza sauce; mix well.

2 Remove 1 crust from pouch; unroll on work surface. With rolling pin, roll into 13-inch round. With 3-inch round cutter, cut out 11 rounds. Repeat with second pie crust.

3 Spoon about 1 teaspoon sausage mixture onto each round. Fold each in half; seal edges with fork. Cut slit in top of each with sharp knife. Place on ungreased large cookie sheet. Brush each foldover with beaten egg.

4 Bake 9 to 11 minutes or until golden brown. Meanwhile, in small saucepan, heat remaining pizza sauce until hot. Serve warm appetizers with warm pizza sauce for dipping.

Make these tasty little morsels ahead of time. Assemble the foldovers and arrange them on a foil-lined cookie sheet; freeze until firm. Place in a resealable freezer plastic bag; freeze up to 2 months. To serve, remove desired number from the bag and bake as directed, increasing baking time if necessary. For a dipping sauce, try additional pizza or pasta sauce, cheese dip or salsa.

High Altitude (3500–6500 ft):
No change.

1 Appetizer: Calories 100 (Calories from Fat 60); Total Fat 6g (Saturated Fat 2g; Trans Fat 0g); Cholesterol 15mg; Sodium 190mg; Total Carbohydrate 11g (Dietary Fiber 0g; Sugars 0g); Protein 1g % Daily Value: Vitamin A 0%; Vitamin C 0%; Calcium 0%; Iron 2% Exchanges: $^1/_2$ Starch, 1 $^1/_2$ Fat Carbohydrate Choices: 1

basil and havarti cheese pinwheels

Prep Time: **20 minutes**   Start to Finish: **40 minutes**   16 appetizers

1 can (8 oz) refrigerated
  crescent dinner rolls
2 tablespoons drained finely
  chopped sun-dried tomatoes
  in oil (from 7-oz jar)
1 package ($2/3$ oz) fresh basil
  leaves (30 to 35 leaves)
$1/2$ cup shredded Havarti
  cheese (2 oz)

1 Heat oven to 350°F. Spray cookie sheet with cooking spray. Unroll dough and separate into 2 long rectangles; press each into 12 × 4-inch rectangle, firmly pressing perforations to seal.

2 Sprinkle tomatoes over each rectangle, spreading evenly. Sprinkle each with basil and cheese.

3 Starting with one short side, roll up each rectangle; press edge to seal. With serrated knife, cut each roll into 8 slices; place cut side down on cookie sheet.

4 Bake 15 to 20 minutes or until edges are golden brown. Immediately remove from cookie sheet. Serve warm.

Havarti is a popular and versatile Danish cheese often used for sandwiches and omelets. It has a buttery, mild yet tangy flavor and a semisoft texture. Brick, Colby or fontina cheese make perfect substitutes.

High Altitude (3500–6500 ft): Bake 13 to 18 minutes.

1 Appetizer: Calories 70 (Calories from Fat 40); Total Fat 4.5g (Saturated Fat 2g; Trans Fat 1g); Cholesterol 0mg; Sodium 140mg; Total Carbohydrate 6g (Dietary Fiber 0g; Sugars 1g); Protein 2g % Daily Value: Vitamin A 2%; Vitamin C 0%; Calcium 2%; Iron 0% Exchanges: $1/2$ Starch, 1 Fat Carbohydrate Choices: $1/2$

bacon-cheddar pinwheels

Prep Time: **15 minutes**   Start to Finish: **35 minutes**   16 appetizers

1 can (8 oz) refrigerated crescent
   dinner rolls
2 tablespoons ranch dressing
1/4 cup cooked real bacon pieces
   or 4 slices bacon, crisply
   cooked, crumbled
1/2 cup finely shredded Cheddar
   cheese (2 oz)
1/4 cup chopped green onions
   (4 medium)

1 Heat oven to 350°F. Unroll dough and separate into 2 long
rectangles; press each into 12 × 4-inch rectangle, firmly pressing
perforations to seal.

2 Spread dressing over each rectangle to edges. Sprinkle each with
bacon, cheese and onions.

3 Starting with one short side, roll up each rectangle; press edge to
seal. With serrated knife, cut each roll into 8 slices; place cut side
down on ungreased cookie sheet.

4 Bake 12 to 17 minutes or until edges are golden brown.
Immediately remove from cookie sheet. Serve warm.

Real bacon pieces are such a time-saver, and
there is no greasy mess! Look for them near the salad
dressing at the grocery store.

High Altitude (3500–6500 ft):
No change.

1 Appetizer: Calories 80 (Calories from Fat 50); Total Fat 6g (Saturated Fat 2g; Trans Fat 1g); Cholesterol 5mg; Sodium
180mg; Total Carbohydrate 6g (Dietary Fiber 0g; Sugars 1g); Protein 2g % Daily Value: Vitamin A 0%; Vitamin C 0%; Calcium
2%; Iron 0% Exchanges: 1/2 Starch, 1 Fat Carbohydrate Choices: 1/2

focaccia dipping sticks

Prep Time: **15 minutes**   Start to Finish: **35 minutes**   28 servings

1 can (13.8 oz) refrigerated
  pizza crust
1 tablespoon extra-virgin
  olive oil
1/3 cup red bell pepper strips
  (1 × 1/8 inch)
3 tablespoons thinly slivered
  pitted ripe olives
1 tablespoon chopped fresh
  rosemary leaves
1/4 teaspoon kosher (coarse) salt
1 cup tomato pasta sauce,
  heated

1 Heat oven to 400°F. Grease cookie sheet with shortening. Unroll dough onto cookie sheet to form 14 × 9-inch rectangle. With fingertips, make indentations over surface of dough.

2 Drizzle oil over dough. Top with remaining ingredients except pasta sauce. Using hands, press toppings gently into dough so they don't fall off when you cut the sticks.

3 Bake 13 to 18 minutes or until golden brown. Remove from cookie sheet. Cut in half lengthwise; cut each half crosswise into 14 sticks. Serve warm sticks with warm pasta sauce for dipping.

Grains of kosher (coarse) salt vary in size depending on the brand. Use less of smaller-grained salt than larger-grained salt. These warm, flavorful breadsticks make a terrific appetizer, or serve them alongside salads and soups.

High Altitude (3500–6500 ft):
No change.

1 Serving: Calories 50 (Calories from Fat 10); Total Fat 1.5g (Saturated Fat 0g; Trans Fat 0g); Cholesterol 0mg; Sodium 170mg; Total Carbohydrate 8g (Dietary Fiber 0g; Sugars 2g); Protein 1g % Daily Value: Vitamin A 0%; Vitamin C 2%; Calcium 0%; Iron 2% Exchanges: 1/2 Starch, 1/2 Fat Carbohydrate Choices: 1/2

celebrate
christmas

Caramel Pecan Sticky Bun Cookies • Rum-Pum-Pum Thumbprints • Mexican Wedding Cakes • Holiday Moments • Chocolate Almond Spritz Wafers • Easy Santa Cookies • Snow Globe Cookie • Spiral Snowmen Cookies • Swirly Tree Cookies • Christmas Ornament Cookies • Cookie Skates • Gingerbread Cookie Wreath • Cream Cheese Sugar Cookies • Mint Brownies Supreme • Raspberry Cheesecake Bars • Ooey Gooey Candy and Chocolate Bars • Heavenly Layered Bars • Scandinavian Almond Bars • White Chocolate–Cranberry-Pecan Tart • Streusel-Topped Cranberry-Pear Tart • Pumpkin Tart with Caramel Rum-Raisin Sauce • Peppermint-Fudge Pie • Tropical Pineapple–Cream Cheese Tart • Classic Pecan Pie • "Gingerbread Boy" Cake • Santa Claus Cake • Chocolate-Cherry Truffle Cake • Cranberry-Orange Pound Cake • Tree-Shaped Brownie Torte • Creamy Cappuccino Cheesecake • Chocolate Bread Pudding with Cherry-Raspberry Sauce • Eggnog Crème Brûlée • Cherry-Cheese Crescent Braid • Cranberry Cream Cheese Swirl Loaf • Mocha Streusel Coffee Cake • Christmas Tree Coffee Cake • Cherry Pistachio Scones • Caramel Sticky Buns • Pesto Angel Wing Rolls • Quick and Easy Onion Rolls • Holiday Biscuit Cutouts • Spinach Dip Crescent Wreath • Savory Crab Cheesecake

caramel pecan sticky bun cookies

Prep Time: **1** hour   Start to Finish: **1** hour   3 dozen cookies

COOKIES

1 cup butter or margarine,
   softened

$1/2$ cup granulated sugar

$1/2$ cup dark corn syrup

2 egg yolks

2 $1/2$ cups all-purpose flour

FILLING

$1/2$ cup powdered sugar

$1/4$ cup butter or margarine

3 tablespoons dark corn syrup

$1/2$ cup coarsely chopped pecans,
   toasted*

1 egg white, slightly beaten

1 In large bowl, beat 1 cup butter and the granulated sugar until light and fluffy. Add $1/2$ cup corn syrup and the egg yolks; blend well. Stir in flour; mix well. Cover with plastic wrap; if necessary, refrigerate 1 hour for easier handling.

2 In small saucepan, mix powdered sugar, $1/4$ cup butter and 3 tablespoons corn syrup; heat to boiling. Remove from heat. Stir in pecans. Refrigerate at least 10 minutes.

3 Meanwhile, heat oven to 375°F. Lightly grease 2 cookie sheets with shortening. Shape dough into 1 $1/2$-inch balls. Place 2 inches apart on cookie sheets. Bake 5 minutes. Brush dough lightly with egg white. With spoon, carefully make deep indentation in center of each cookie; fill each with $1/2$ teaspoon filling. Bake 6 to 9 minutes longer or until light golden brown. Cool 1 to 2 minutes; remove from cookie sheets. Cool completely.

*To toast pecans, bake uncovered in ungreased shallow pan in 350°F oven 6 to 10 minutes, stirring occasionally, until light brown.

Buttery, rich, and so good—just looking at one of these cookies will go straight to your hips! Arrange these cookies on disposable decorative platters and wrap with fun seasonal theme-print plastic wrap for awesome gifts.

High Altitude (3500–6500 ft): Decrease butter in cookies to $3/4$ cup; decrease corn syrup in cookies to $1/3$ cup. Bake on ungreased cookie sheets.

1 Cookie: Calories 140 (Calories from Fat 70); Total Fat 8g (Saturated Fat 4g; Trans Fat 0g); Cholesterol 30mg; Sodium 55mg; Total Carbohydrate 16g (Dietary Fiber 0g; Sugars 7g); Protein 1g % Daily Value: Vitamin A 4%; Vitamin C 0%; Calcium 0%; Iron 2% Exchanges: $1/2$ Starch, $1/2$ Other Carbohydrate, 1 $1/2$ Fat Carbohydrate Choices: 1

rum-pum-pum thumbprints

Prep Time: **1 hour 10 minutes** Start to Finish: **2 hours 10 minutes** *4 ¹/₂ dozen cookies*

COOKIES

1 cup butter or margarine,
   softened

¹/₂ cup packed brown sugar

1 egg

2 teaspoons vanilla

2 teaspoons rum extract

2 cups all-purpose flour

1 teaspoon ground nutmeg

FROSTING

2 cups powdered sugar

3 tablespoons butter or
   margarine, softened

¹/₂ teaspoon rum extract

2 to 3 tablespoons milk

Food color, if desired

1 In large bowl, beat 1 cup butter and the brown sugar until light and fluffy. Add egg, vanilla and 2 teaspoons rum extract; blend well. Stir in flour and nutmeg; mix well. Cover with plastic wrap; refrigerate 1 hour for easier handling.

2 Heat oven to 325°F. Shape dough into 1-inch balls; place 2 inches apart on ungreased cookie sheets. With thumb, make imprint in center of each cookie.

3 Bake 11 to 14 minutes or until firm to the touch. Cool 1 minute; remove from cookie sheets.

4 In small bowl, blend all frosting ingredients until smooth, adding enough milk for desired spreading consistency. Spoon or pipe about ¹/₂ teaspoon frosting into center of each cookie.

These rum cookies would go perfectly with mugs of eggnog.

High Altitude (3500–6500 ft): Increase flour to 2 ¹/₄ cups.

1 Cookie: Calories 80 (Calories from Fat 40); Total Fat 4g (Saturated Fat 2.5g; Trans Fat 0g); Cholesterol 15mg; Sodium 30mg; Total Carbohydrate 10g (Dietary Fiber 0g; Sugars 6g); Protein 0g % Daily Value: Vitamin A 2%; Vitamin C 0%; Calcium 0%; Iron 0% Exchanges: ¹/₂ Other Carbohydrate, 1 Fat Carbohydrate Choices: ¹/₂

mexican wedding cakes

1 $^1/_4$ cups powdered sugar

1 cup butter or margarine,
    softened

2 teaspoons vanilla

2 cups all-purpose flour

1 cup finely chopped or ground
    almonds or pecans

$^1/_4$ teaspoon salt

1 Heat oven to 325°F. In large bowl, beat $^1/_2$ cup of the powdered sugar, the butter and vanilla with electric mixer on medium speed, scraping bowl occasionally, until light and fluffy. On low speed, beat in flour, almonds and salt, scraping bowl occasionally, until well combined.

2 Shape dough into 1-inch balls; place 1 inch apart on ungreased cookie sheets.

3 Bake 13 to 17 minutes or until set but not brown. Immediately remove from cookie sheets; place on cooling racks. Cool slightly, about 10 minutes.

4 Roll cookies in remaining $^3/_4$ cup powdered sugar; return to cooling racks. Cool completely, about 15 minutes. Reroll cookies in powdered sugar.

Shape these all-time favorites into balls, crescents or small logs. For a fun tweak, dip them into melted chocolate instead of the powdered sugar.

High Altitude (3500–6500 ft):
No change.

1 Cookie: Calories 70 (Calories from Fat 40); Total Fat 4.5g (Saturated Fat 2.5g; Trans Fat 0g); Cholesterol 10mg; Sodium 35mg; Total Carbohydrate 7g (Dietary Fiber 0g; Sugars 3g); Protein 1g % Daily Value: Vitamin A 2%; Vitamin C 0%; Calcium 0%; Iron 0% Exchanges: $^1/_2$ Other Carbohydrate, 1 Fat Carbohydrate Choices: $^1/_2$

holiday moments

Prep Time: **1 hour**   Start to Finish: **2 hours**   3 dozen cookies

1 cup butter or margarine,
    softened

$^3/_4$ cup cornstarch

$^1/_3$ cup powdered sugar

1 cup all-purpose flour

3 tablespoons powdered sugar

2 tablespoons red decorator
    sugar crystals

2 tablespoons green decorator
    sugar crystals

1 In large bowl, beat butter with electric mixer until light and fluffy. Add cornstarch and $^1/_3$ cup powdered sugar; beat on low speed until moistened. Beat on high speed until light and fluffy. Add flour; mix until dough forms. Cover with plastic wrap; refrigerate at least 1 hour for easier handling.

2 Heat oven to 350°F. Shape dough into 1-inch balls; place 1 inch apart on ungreased cookie sheets.

3 Bake 9 to 15 minutes or until cookies are very light golden brown. Cool 1 minute; remove from cookie sheets.

4 In small bowl, mix 3 tablespoons powdered sugar and both decorator sugars; carefully roll warm cookies in mixture.

Cornstarch in cookie dough? Yes, it provides structure without the gluten that flour has, so the result is a cookie with a very tender, almost fragile texture.

High Altitude (3500–6500 ft):
Increase flour to 1 $^1/_4$ cups.

1 Cookie: Calories 80 (Calories from Fat 45); Total Fat 5g (Saturated Fat 3g; Trans Fat 0g); Cholesterol 15mg; Sodium 35mg; Total Carbohydrate 8g (Dietary Fiber 0g; Sugars 3g); Protein 0g % Daily Value: Vitamin A 4%; Vitamin C 0%; Calcium 0%; Iron 0% Exchanges: $^1/_2$ Other Carbohydrate, 1 Fat Carbohydrate Choices: $^1/_2$

chocolate almond spritz wafers

Prep Time: **1 hour 30 minutes**   Start to Finish: **1 hour 30 minutes**   8 dozen cookies

COOKIES

1 cup powdered sugar

1 cup butter or margarine,
   softened

1 egg

1 teaspoon almond extract

2 $1/3$ cups all-purpose flour

$1/2$ teaspoon salt

GLAZE

8 oz semisweet baking
   chocolate, cut into pieces

2 tablespoons shortening

Sliced almonds

1 Heat oven to 400°F. In large bowl, beat powdered sugar and butter until light and fluffy. Add egg and almond extract; blend well. Stir in flour and salt; mix well. Fill cookie press with dough. Using the bar plate, form 4 strips of dough the length of ungreased cookie sheet. Score cookie dough at 2 $1/2$-inch intervals.

2 Bake 3 to 5 minutes or until set but not brown. Cut strips into individual cookies on scored lines. Immediately remove from cookie sheet. Cool completely.

3 Line cookie sheets with waxed paper. In small saucepan, melt chocolate and shortening over low heat, stirring constantly. Remove from heat. Set saucepan in hot water to maintain dipping consistency.

4 Dip half of cooled cookie into chocolate; allow excess to drip off. Place cookies on cookie sheet. Sprinkle or arrange almond slices over chocolate. Let stand until glaze is set. Store between sheets of waxed paper in loosely covered container.

Variety is the spice of life! Instead of dipping the
   ends of these cookies just in semisweet chocolate, try
   exploring bittersweet, white and milk chocolate too!

High Altitude (3500–6500 ft):
No change.

1 Cookie: Calories 50 (Calories from Fat 30); Total Fat 3g (Saturated Fat 1.5g; Trans Fat 0g); Cholesterol 5mg; Sodium 25mg; Total Carbohydrate 5g (Dietary Fiber 0g; Sugars 2g); Protein 0g % Daily Value: Vitamin A 0%; Vitamin C 0%; Calcium 0%; Iron 0% Exchanges: $1/2$ Other Carbohydrate, $1/2$ Fat Carbohydrate Choices: $1/2$

easy santa cookies

| Prep Time: **1 hour** | Start to Finish: **2 hours** | 34 cookies |

COOKIES

1 roll (16.5 oz) refrigerated sugar
   cookies

FROSTING

2 cups powdered sugar

2 tablespoons butter or
   margarine, softened

2 to 3 tablespoons milk

2 to 3 drops red food color

DECORATIONS

68 semisweet chocolate chips
   (about ¹/₄ cup)

34 red cinnamon candies

²/₃ cup coconut

34 miniature marshmallows

1 Freeze cookie dough at least 1 hour.

2 Heat oven to 350°F. Cut frozen dough into ¹/₄-inch slices. (Return dough to freezer if it becomes too soft to cut.) Place slices 3 inches apart on ungreased cookie sheets. Bake 8 to 12 minutes or until golden brown. Cool 2 minutes; remove from cookie sheets. Cool completely.

3 Meanwhile, in small bowl, beat powdered sugar, butter and enough milk for desired spreading consistency until smooth. In another small bowl, place half of frosting. Add red food color; stir until blended.

4 Frost cooled cookies with red and white frosting. Use small amount of frosting to attach chocolate chips for eyes and cinnamon candy for nose. Gently press coconut into white frosting for beard. Press marshmallow into red frosting for tassel on cap. Let stand until frosting is set. Store between sheets of waxed paper in tightly covered container.

For a great stocking stuffer, make Santa Cookie Pops: insert a wooden stick with rounded ends or cookie stick halfway into each cookie before baking. Wrap finished "pops" with colored plastic wrap, leaving the stick unwrapped, and tie with ribbon.

High Altitude (3500–6500 ft):
No change.

1 Cookie: Calories 110 (Calories from Fat 40); Total Fat 4g (Saturated Fat 2g; Trans Fat 0.5g); Cholesterol 5mg; Sodium 45mg; Total Carbohydrate 18g (Dietary Fiber 0g; Sugars 13g); Protein 0g % Daily Value: Vitamin A 0%; Vitamin C 0%; Calcium 0%; Iron 2% Exchanges: 1 Other Carbohydrate, 1 Fat Carbohydrate Choices: 1

snow globe cookie

| Prep Time: **55 minutes** | Start to Finish: **1 hour 25 minutes** | 16 servings |

1/4 cup all-purpose flour

1 roll (16.5 oz) refrigerated sugar
  cookies

1 container (1 lb) vanilla creamy
  ready-to-spread frosting

5 drops green food color

10 drops blue food color

Assorted small candy sprinkles,
  edible glitter and/or decorator
  sugar

Let your creativity shine
when decorating the
snowman and trees on this
large cookie. Miniature
chocolate chips, candy-
coated chocolate candies,
colored sugar and candy
sprinkles are just a few
decorative candies to try.

1 Heat oven to 350°F. Line large cookie sheet with foil. Sprinkle flour over work surface. Cut roll of cookie dough in half crosswise. Return 1 half to refrigerator.

2 To form top of globe, shape dough into ball; roll in flour to coat. Place on one end of cookie sheet. Press or roll into 10-inch round.

3 Cut remaining dough in half. To form base of globe, shape 1 half into ball; roll in flour to coat. Press or roll into 8-inch round. Cut round in half; place half round next to 10-inch round on foil-lined cookie sheet, rounded edges touching.

4 Bake 7 to 11 minutes or until light golden brown. Cool completely, about 30 minutes. Carefully peel foil from back of cookie; place cookie on tray or foil-covered cardboard.

5 Meanwhile, grease cookie sheet with shortening. Coat remaining dough with flour; roll to 1/8-inch thickness. With floured cookie cutters, cut two 3 1/2- to 4-inch trees, one 2-inch tree, one 3 1/2- to 4-inch snowman and three 1 1/4-inch stars. Bake stars 2 to 3 minutes; trees and snowman 7 to 10 minutes or until light golden brown. Cool 1 minute; remove from cookie sheet. Cool completely, about 30 minutes.

6 Use 1/3 cup vanilla frosting to frost base of globe. Frost stars and snowman with vanilla frosting. In small bowl, blend 2 tablespoons frosting and the green food color. Frost trees. To remaining frosting, add blue food color; blend well. Frost globe and decorate as shown in photo.

High Altitude (3500–6500 ft): In large bowl, break up cookie dough. Stir or knead in 1/4 cup all-purpose flour. Reshape into 8-inch roll. Continue as directed in step 1.

1 Serving: Calories 260 (Calories from Fat 110); Total Fat 12g (Saturated Fat 3g; Trans Fat 3.5g); Cholesterol 10mg; Sodium 150mg; Total Carbohydrate 38g (Dietary Fiber 0g; Sugars 26g); Protein 1g % Daily Value: Vitamin A 0%; Vitamin C 0%; Calcium 0%; Iron 2% Exchanges: 2 1/2 Other Carbohydrate, 2 1/2 Fat Carbohydrate Choices: 2 1/2

spiral snowmen cookies

extra easy

Prep Time: **1 hour**   Start to Finish: **1 hour 10 minutes**   20 cookies

1 roll (16.5 oz) refrigerated sugar
   cookies
2 tablespoons all-purpose flour
Large gumdrops
Miniature candy-coated
   chocolate baking bits
Miniature chocolate chips
Coarse sugar

1 Heat oven to 350°F. In large bowl, break up cookie dough. Stir or knead in flour until well blended. Divide dough in half; wrap each half in plastic wrap. Freeze 10 minutes.

2 Shape half of dough into 1 1/2-inch balls. With fingers, roll each ball into 10-inch rope, about 1/4 inch wide; carefully place on ungreased cookie sheet. With each rope, starting at top, make small spiral for head, continuing to make larger spiral for body. (See photo.)

3 Cut hat shapes from gumdrops; place on heads. Use baking bits for buttons; use miniature chocolate chips for eyes and noses. Cut small pieces from red gumdrop for mouths. Sprinkle with coarse sugar. Repeat with remaining half of dough.

4 Bake 9 to 13 minutes or until edges are light golden brown. Cool 1 minute; remove from cookie sheet to cooling rack.

For Spiral Snowman on a Stick, just place a flat wooden stick in the bottom of each cookie before baking.

High Altitude (3500–6500 ft): Bake 14 to 18 minutes.

1 Undecorated Cookie: Calories 110 (Calories from Fat 45); Total Fat 5g (Saturated Fat 1g; Trans Fat 1g); Cholesterol 10mg; Sodium 65mg; Total Carbohydrate 15g (Dietary Fiber 0g; Sugars 8g); Protein 0g % Daily Value: Vitamin A 0%; Vitamin C 0%; Calcium 0%; Iron 0% Exchanges: 1 Other Carbohydrate, 1 Fat Carbohydrate Choices: 1

swirly tree cookies

extra easy

Prep Time: **1 hour 5 minutes**   Start to Finish: **1 hour 15 minutes**   16 large cookies

1 roll (16.5 oz) refrigerated sugar
  cookies
2 tablespoons all-purpose flour
Green food color
Assorted small candies

1 Heat oven to 350°F. In large bowl, break up cookie dough. Stir or knead in flour until well blended. Knead in enough food color until well blended and desired green color. Divide dough in half; wrap each half in plastic wrap. Freeze 10 minutes.

2 Shape half of dough into 1 1/2-inch balls. With fingers, roll each ball into 10-inch rope, about 1/4 inch wide; break off small piece from each rope for tree trunk. Carefully place ropes on ungreased cookie sheet. With each rope, starting at top, twist rope back and forth into tree shape, gradually making larger at bottom (rows of dough should touch). If rope breaks, press dough together. Place small piece at bottom of each tree for trunk. Repeat with remaining half of dough.

3 Decorate trees with candies to resemble ornaments and lights. If desired, place 1 candy at top of tree for star.

4 Bake 9 to 13 minutes or until edges are light golden brown. Cool 1 minute; remove from cookie sheet.

To easily mix the food color into the dough, put both in a large resealable food-storage plastic bag. Seal and knead until it's all blended.

High Altitude (3500–6500 ft):
No change.

1 Large Cookie: Calories 150 (Calories from Fat 60); Total Fat 6g (Saturated Fat 2g; Trans Fat 1.5g); Cholesterol 10mg; Sodium 80mg; Total Carbohydrate 21g (Dietary Fiber 0g; Sugars 12g); Protein 1g % Daily Value: Vitamin A 0%; Vitamin C 0%; Calcium 0%; Iron 4% Exchanges: 1/2 Starch, 1 Other Carbohydrate, 1 Fat Carbohydrate Choices: 1 1/2

all wrapped up

The possibilities for packaging holiday goodies are endless! These ideas for festive containers and wrappings will help you create personalized, one-of-a-kind gifts sure to bring plenty of holiday cheer.

Make oversized latte bowls or coffee mugs or large plastic decorative goblets or drink glasses do double duty as cookie holders.

Put breads and cakes in fun seasonal printed cardboard or plastic containers or gift bags.

Recycle creatively: dress up outside of plastic, metal or glass jars and canisters with colorful felt, or felt cutouts or wrapping paper.

Customize! Finish your container with ribbon, bows, ID cards, and little extras to go with the gift like coffee, tea, cookie cutters, recipe cards, measuring spoons, pie servers or even a pretty serving piece.

christmas ornament cookies

Prep Time: **1 hour** | Start to Finish: **1 hour 30 minutes** | 2 dozen cookies

1 roll (16.5 oz) refrigerated sugar cookies

1 egg white, beaten

1 tablespoon red sugar

1 tablespoon green sugar

12 small gumdrops, cut in half

1 Heat oven to 350°F. Cut cookie dough lengthwise into 3 long slices (see diagram); separate slices on work surface with rounded sides down. Lightly brush all cut surfaces with egg white.

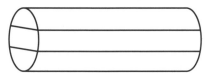

2 Sprinkle egg white area of 1 rounded slice with red sugar. Place middle slice on top; sprinkle with green sugar. Place remaining rounded slice, egg white side down, on top; press firmly and if necessary, reshape into roll. Wrap roll in plastic wrap; freeze 30 minutes.

Waxed paper makes cleanup a breeze. In step 1, put the long cookie slices on waxed paper— no messy countertops!

3 Cut roll into 24 slices; place slices 1 inch apart on ungreased cookie sheets.

4 Bake 9 to 11 minutes or until edges are light golden brown. Immediately press gumdrop half onto outer edge of each cookie to resemble ornament hanger. Cool 2 minutes; remove from cookie sheets.

High Altitude (3500–6500 ft): No change.

1 Cookie: Calories 90 (Calories from Fat 35); Total Fat 3.5g (Saturated Fat 1g; Trans Fat 1g); Cholesterol 5mg; Sodium 55mg; Total Carbohydrate 14g (Dietary Fiber 0g; Sugars 8g); Protein 0g % Daily Value: Vitamin A 0%; Vitamin C 0%; Calcium 0%; Iron 2% Exchanges: $^{1}/_{2}$ Starch, $^{1}/_{2}$ Other Carbohydrate, $^{1}/_{2}$ Fat Carbohydrate Choices: 1

cookie skates

extra
easy

Prep Time: **1 hour 20 minutes**   Start to Finish: **1 hour 50 minutes**   30 cookies

---

COOKIES

$^1/_2$ roll (16.5-oz size) refrigerated
   sugar cookies

$^1/_4$ cup all-purpose flour

FROSTING

1 $^1/_2$ cups powdered sugar

$^1/_4$ cup butter or margarine,
   softened

4 to 6 teaspoons lemon juice

Green food color

30 small candy canes

These are great cookies
to make in stages. One day,
shape and bake the cookies.
Cool completely and freeze
in a tightly covered container
up to 1 month ahead of time.
Another day, thaw, frost and
decorate the cookies.

1 In large bowl, break up cookie dough. Add flour; mix with hands until well blended. Shape dough into 10-inch log; wrap in plastic wrap. Freeze 30 minutes.

2 Heat oven to 350°F. Remove dough from freezer. Flatten dough down center with handle of wooden spoon. To form boot shape, with fingers, flatten one side of log until about $^3/_4$ inch thick. (See photo.) Cut log into $^3/_8$-inch-thick slices; place on ungreased cookie sheets. Flatten slightly with fingers.

3 Bake 8 to 11 minutes or until edges are light golden brown. Immediately remove from cookie sheets. Cool completely, about 15 minutes.

4 In small bowl, mix powdered sugar, butter and enough lemon juice for desired spreading consistency. In another small bowl, reserve $^1/_3$ of frosting; add green food color and blend well. Place green frosting in resealable food-storage plastic bag; cut off one small corner of bag.

5 Frost cookies with white frosting. Place small amount of white frosting along bottom edge of each cookie; attach candy canes to form "skate blades," breaking off portion of tip on curved end, if necessary. With green frosting, pipe laces and bows on skates.

High Altitude (3500–6500 ft):
No change.

1 Cookie: Calories 90 (Calories from Fat 25); Total Fat 3g (Saturated Fat 1.5g; Trans Fat 0g); Cholesterol 5mg; Sodium 35mg; Total Carbohydrate 14g (Dietary Fiber 0g; Sugars 11g); Protein 0g % Daily Value: Vitamin A 0%; Vitamin C 0%; Calcium 0%; Iron 0% Exchanges: $^1/_2$ Starch, $^1/_2$ Other Carbohydrate, $^1/_2$ Fat Carbohydrate Choices: 1

gingerbread cookie wreath

Prep Time: **1 hour 40 minutes**	Start to Finish: **1 hour 40 minutes**	16 servings

3 tablespoons all-purpose flour

1 roll (16.5 oz) refrigerated
   gingerbread cookies

2 cups powdered sugar

3 to 4 tablespoons water or milk

Food color

Assorted small candy sprinkles,
   edible glitter and/or
   decorator sugar

1 Heat oven to 350°F. Line cookie sheet with parchment paper. Draw 10-inch circle on paper. Turn paper over so mark is on underside; line will show through.

2 Sprinkle 1 tablespoon of the flour on work surface. Shape $^1/_3$ of the cookie dough into ball; press into flour. Keep remaining dough refrigerated. Press dough to form 6-inch round, turning and coating with flour frequently. Place in center of circle on cookie sheet. Roll to form 10-inch round, about $^1/_4$ inch thick. If necessary, trim uneven edges. Cut 4-inch round from center; remove smaller dough round and set aside for cut-out cookies.

3 Bake wreath 7 to 9 minutes or until light golden brown. Remove from cookie sheet; place on cooling rack. Cool completely.

4 Meanwhile, roll half of remaining dough on floured surface to $^1/_4$-inch thickness. With $1^1/_2$- to 3-inch Christmas cookie cutters, cut out shapes. Place on ungreased cookie sheets. Repeat with remaining half of dough, dough scraps and flour.

5 Bake shapes 7 to 9 minutes or until light golden brown. Remove from cookie sheets; place on cooling racks. Cool completely.

6 In small bowl, blend powdered sugar and enough water for desired spreading consistency. Divide frosting into small bowls; add food color as desired. Frost and decorate cookies as desired. With dabs of frosting, attach cut-out cookies to cookie wreath, allowing 1 layer to set before adding another layer.

High Altitude (3500–6500 ft):
No change.

1 Serving without Decorations: Calories 200 (Calories from Fat 60); Total Fat 7g (Saturated Fat 1.5g; Trans Fat 2g); Cholesterol 15mg; Sodium 100mg; Total Carbohydrate 33g (Dietary Fiber 0g; Sugars 23g); Protein 2g % Daily Value: Vitamin A 0%; Vitamin C 0%; Calcium 0%; Iron 4% Exchanges: $^1/_2$ Starch, $1^1/_2$ Other Carbohydrate, $1^1/_2$ Fat Carbohydrate Choices: 2

For a delightfully delicious centerpiece, put the wreath on a large flat platter or mirror. Arrange a short candle or several votives inside the wreath.

cream cheese sugar cookies

Prep Time: **1 hour**	Start to Finish: **2 hours**	6 dozen cookies

1 cup sugar

1 cup butter or margarine,
   softened

1 package (3 oz) cream cheese,
   softened

$1/2$ teaspoon salt

$1/2$ teaspoon almond extract

$1/2$ teaspoon vanilla

1 egg yolk

2 cups all-purpose flour

Colored sugar or decorating
   icing, if desired

1 In large bowl, beat all ingredients except flour and colored sugar until light and fluffy. Add flour; mix well. Shape dough into 3 disks. Wrap dough in plastic wrap; refrigerate 1 hour for easier handling.

2 Heat oven to 375°F. On floured work surface, roll out 1 disk of dough at a time to $1/8$-inch thickness. (Keep remaining dough refrigerated.) Cut with lightly floured 2 $1/2$-inch round or desired shape cookie cutters. Place 1 inch apart on ungreased cookie sheets. Decorate with colored sugar.

3 Bake 6 to 10 minutes or until light golden brown. Immediately remove from cookie sheets. If desired, frost and decorate plain cookies.

The cream cheese in this classic sugar cookie recipe makes the dough extra tender. To quickly soften the cream cheese, remove the wrapper and place it in a microwavable glass bowl. Microwave on Medium (50%) 45 to 60 seconds or until softened.

High Altitude (3500–6500 ft):
Increase flour to 2 $1/4$ cups.

1 Cookie without Decorations: Calories 50 (Calories from Fat 30); Total Fat 3g (Saturated Fat 2g; Trans Fat 0g); Cholesterol 10mg; Sodium 40mg; Total Carbohydrate 5g (Dietary Fiber 0g; Sugars 3g); Protein 0g % Daily Value: Vitamin A 0%; Vitamin C 0%; Calcium 0%; Iron 0% Exchanges: $1/2$ Other Carbohydrate, $1/2$ Fat Carbohydrate Choices: $1/2$

mint brownies supreme

Prep Time: **15 minutes**   Start to Finish: **3 hours 30 minutes**   48 brownies

BROWNIES

1 box (1 lb 3.8 oz) fudge brownie
mix

$^1/_2$ cup vegetable oil

$^1/_4$ cup water

2 eggs

FILLING

$^1/_2$ cup butter or margarine,
softened

1 package (3 oz) cream cheese,
softened

2 $^1/_2$ cups powdered sugar

3 tablespoons crème de menthe
syrup

Green food color, if desired

FROSTING

1 bag (6 oz) semisweet
chocolate chips (1 cup)

$^1/_3$ cup butter or margarine

1 Heat oven to 350°F. Grease bottom only of 13 × 9-inch pan with shortening. In medium bowl, stir brownie mix, oil, water and eggs with spoon until well blended. Spread in pan.

2 Bake 28 to 30 minutes or until set. DO NOT OVERBAKE. Cool completely.

3 In medium bowl, beat $^1/_2$ cup butter and the cream cheese until light and fluffy. Add remaining filling ingredients; beat until smooth. Spread evenly over cooled brownies.

4 In small saucepan, melt frosting ingredients over low heat, stirring constantly, until smooth. Remove from heat; cool 15 minutes. Pour frosting evenly over filling; spread carefully to cover. Refrigerate 1 hour before cutting. For brownies, cut into 6 rows by 8 rows. Store in refrigerator.

You'll find crème de menthe syrup in the ice cream topping section of your supermarket. Stronger-tasting crème de menthe liqueur can be substituted for the syrup.

High Altitude (3500–6500 ft): Add $^1/_4$ cup all-purpose flour to dry brownie mix.

1 Brownie: Calories 150 (Calories from Fat 70); Total Fat 8g (Saturated Fat 3.5g; Trans Fat 0g); Cholesterol 20mg; Sodium 75mg; Total Carbohydrate 19g (Dietary Fiber 0g; Sugars 16g); Protein 0g % Daily Value: Vitamin A 2%; Vitamin C 0%; Calcium 0%; Iron 2% Exchanges: $^1/_2$ Starch, $^1/_2$ Other Carbohydrate, 1 $^1/_2$ Fat Carbohydrate Choices: 1

raspberry cheesecake bars

Prep Time: **20 minutes**   Start to Finish: **1 hour 55 minutes**   25 bars

CRUST

$^1/_2$ cup sugar

$^1/_2$ cup butter or margarine, softened

1 $^1/_4$ cups all-purpose flour

FILLING

1 package (8 oz) cream cheese, softened

$^1/_2$ cup sugar

$^1/_2$ teaspoon almond extract

1 egg

TOPPING

4 tablespoons seedless red raspberry jam

1 Heat oven to 350°F. Spray 9-inch square pan with cooking spray. In large bowl, mix $^1/_2$ cup sugar and the butter until well blended. Stir in flour until crumbly. Press mixture in bottom of pan.

2 Bake 15 to 18 minutes or until edges are light golden brown. Meanwhile, in large bowl, beat all filling ingredients with electric mixer until well blended. Pour filling over partially baked crust. In small bowl, stir 2 tablespoons of the jam until softened. Spoon over cream cheese mixture. With tip of spoon, carefully swirl jam into top of filling (do not disturb crust).

3 Bake 15 to 20 minutes longer or until filling is set. Cool 30 minutes.

4 Stir remaining 2 tablespoons jam until smooth; spread evenly over cooled bars. Refrigerate 30 minutes. For bars, cut into 5 rows by 5 rows. Store in refrigerator.

For easier swirling and spreading, give jam a jump start in the microwave. In microwavable dish, microwave jam on High 10 to 15 seconds or just until it's warm, then stir.

High Altitude (3500–6500 ft): In step 2, bake 18 to 21 minutes.

1 Bar: Calories 130 (Calories from Fat 60); Total Fat 7g (Saturated Fat 4.5g; Trans Fat 0g); Cholesterol 30mg; Sodium 55mg; Total Carbohydrate 15g (Dietary Fiber 0g; Sugars 10g); Protein 2g % Daily Value: Vitamin A 4%; Vitamin C 0%; Calcium 0%; Iron 2% Exchanges: $^1/_2$ Starch, $^1/_2$ Other Carbohydrate, 1 $^1/_2$ Fat Carbohydrate Choices: 1

ooey gooey candy and chocolate bars

Prep Time: 15 minutes   Start to Finish: 1 hour 35 minutes   24 bars

1 roll (16.5 oz) refrigerated
   chocolate chip cookies

1 cup quick-cooking oats

10 caramels, unwrapped

1 tablespoon milk

1 cup miniature marshmallows

$1/_3$ cup candy-coated chocolate
   candies

1 Heat oven to 350°F. Spray 8-inch square pan with cooking spray. In medium bowl, break up cookie dough. Stir in oats. Press dough evenly in pan to form crust. Bake 15 to 20 minutes or until golden brown.

2 Meanwhile, in 1-quart saucepan, heat caramels and milk over low heat, stirring frequently, until caramels are melted and smooth. Remove from heat.

3 Sprinkle marshmallows evenly over warm crust; bake 1 to 2 minutes longer or until marshmallows are puffy. Drizzle melted caramels evenly over warm bars; sprinkle with chocolate candies. Cool completely on cooling rack, about 1 hour. For bars, cut into 6 rows by 4 rows with hot, wet knife.

To grab a handful of caramels for this recipe without buying a whole bag, check out the bulk candy section of the store for individually wrapped caramels and buy just 10.

High Altitude (3500–6500 ft): In step 1, bake 19 to 24 minutes.

1 Bar: Calories 140 (Calories from Fat 50); Total Fat 6g (Saturated Fat 2g; Trans Fat 0.5g); Cholesterol 0mg; Sodium 75mg; Total Carbohydrate 21g (Dietary Fiber 0g; Sugars 12g); Protein 2g % Daily Value: Vitamin A 0%; Vitamin C 0%; Calcium 0%; Iron 4% Exchanges: $1/_2$ Starch, 1 Other Carbohydrate, 1 Fat Carbohydrate Choices: 1 $1/_2$

heavenly layered bars

Prep Time: **10 minutes**   Start to Finish: **2 hours 50 minutes**   36 bars

1 roll (16.5 oz) refrigerated
   chocolate chip cookies

$1/2$ cup chocolate cookie crumbs

1 bag (11 oz) butterscotch chips

1 $1/2$ cups flaked coconut

$1/2$ cup chopped walnuts

1 can (14 oz) sweetened
   condensed milk (not
   evaporated)

1 Heat oven to 350°F. Line 13 × 9-inch pan with heavy-duty foil, extending foil over sides of pan. Spray bottom and sides of foil with cooking spray or grease foil with shortening. Break up cookie dough into pan. With floured fingers, press dough evenly in bottom of pan to form crust.

2 Sprinkle cookie crumbs evenly over crust. Top evenly with butterscotch chips, coconut and walnuts. Drizzle with condensed milk.

3 Bake 30 to 40 minutes or until edges are golden brown. (Center will not be set.) Cool completely, about 2 hours. Use foil to lift bars from pan. For bars, cut into 6 rows by 6 rows.

Give these super simple bars a special twist by cutting them into diamonds instead of squares or rectangles—a festive addition to any holiday cookie tray.

High Altitude (3500–6500 ft): No change.

1 Bar: Calories 180 (Calories from Fat 80); Total Fat 9g (Saturated Fat 4.5g; Trans Fat 0.5g); Cholesterol 5mg; Sodium 80mg; Total Carbohydrate 22g (Dietary Fiber 0g; Sugars 18g); Protein 2g % Daily Value: Vitamin A 0%; Vitamin C 0%; Calcium 4%; Iron 2% Exchanges: $1/2$ Starch, 1 Other Carbohydrate, 2 Fat Carbohydrate Choices: 1 $1/2$

scandinavian almond bars

Prep Time: **10 minutes** Start to Finish: **1 hour 5 minutes** 48 bars

1 roll (16.5 oz) refrigerated sugar
  cookies

$^1/_2$ teaspoon ground cinnamon

1 teaspoon almond extract

1 egg white

1 tablespoon water

1 cup sliced almonds

$^1/_4$ cup sugar

1 Heat oven to 350°F. Grease 15 × 10 × 1-inch pan with shortening. In large bowl, break up cookie dough. Add cinnamon and almond extract; mix well. With floured fingers, press dough mixture evenly in bottom of pan.

2 In small bowl, beat egg white and water until frothy. Brush over dough. Sprinkle evenly with almonds and sugar.

3 Bake 17 to 22 minutes or until edges are golden brown. Cool completely, about 30 minutes. For diamond-shaped bars, cut 5 straight parallel lines about 1 $^1/_2$ inches apart down length of pan; cut diagonal lines about 1 $^1/_2$ inches apart across straight lines.

Almond-lovers would so appreciate getting
a pan of these bars as a gift. Package the bars with
almond-flavored coffee or tea to make it extra-special.

High Altitude (3500–6500 ft): 1 Bar: Calories 60 (Calories from Fat 25); Total Fat 3g (Saturated Fat 0.5g; Trans Fat 0g); Cholesterol 5mg; Sodium 25mg;
No change. Total Carbohydrate 7g (Dietary Fiber 0g; Sugars 4g); Protein 0g % Daily Value: Vitamin A 0%; Vitamin C 0%; Calcium 0%;
Iron 0% Exchanges: $^1/_2$ Other Carbohydrate, $^1/_2$ Fat Carbohydrate Choices: $^1/_2$

white chocolate–cranberry-pecan tart

| Prep Time: **30 minutes** | Start to Finish: **3 hours 15 minutes** | 12 servings |

CRUST

1 refrigerated pie crust (from 15-oz box), softened as directed on box

FILLING

1 cup fresh or frozen cranberries

1 cup pecan halves

1 cup white vanilla baking chips

3 eggs

³/₄ cup packed brown sugar

³/₄ cup light corn syrup

2 tablespoons all-purpose flour

1 teaspoon grated orange peel

TOPPING

Whipped cream, if desired

1 Place cookie sheet in oven on middle oven rack. Heat oven to 400°F. Place pie crust in 10-inch tart pan with removable bottom as directed on box for One-Crust Filled Pie.*

2 Layer cranberries, pecans and baking chips in crust-lined pan. In large bowl, beat eggs. Add brown sugar, corn syrup, flour and orange peel; blend well. Pour over cranberry mixture.

3 Place tart on cookie sheet in oven. Bake 25 minutes. Cover tart loosely with foil lightly sprayed with cooking spray; bake 10 to 20 minutes longer or until crust is golden brown and filling is set in center. Remove foil; cool completely, about 2 hours. Serve with whipped cream. Store in refrigerator.

*This dessert can be made in a 9-inch glass pie plate. When mixing the filling, increase the flour to 3 tablespoons.

No white vanilla baking chips? Semisweet chocolate chips can be substituted and would taste divine in this festive tart.

High Altitude (3500–6500 ft): In step 3, after adding foil bake 10 to 15 minutes longer.

1 Serving: Calories 390 (Calories from Fat 160); Total Fat 17g (Saturated Fat 7g; Trans Fat 0g); Cholesterol 55mg; Sodium 160mg; Total Carbohydrate 54g (Dietary Fiber 1g; Sugars 34g); Protein 4g % Daily Value: Vitamin A 0%; Vitamin C 0%; Calcium 6%; Iron 4% Exchanges: 1 Starch, 2 ¹/₂ Other Carbohydrate, 3 ¹/₂ Fat Carbohydrate Choices: 3 ¹/₂

streusel-topped cranberry-pear tart

Prep Time: **25 minutes**   Start to Finish: **1 hour 20 minutes**   8 servings

CRUST

1 refrigerated pie crust (from 15-oz box), softened as directed on box

FILLING

$1/2$ cup sugar

4 teaspoons cornstarch

2 teaspoons ground cinnamon

4 cups thinly sliced peeled pears

$3/4$ cup fresh or frozen cranberries

TOPPING

$1/4$ cup sugar

$1/4$ cup all-purpose flour

2 tablespoons butter or margarine, softened

1. Place cookie sheet in oven on middle oven rack. Heat oven to 375°F. Place pie crust in 9-inch tart pan with removable bottom as directed on box for One-Crust Filled Pie.

2. In large bowl, mix $1/2$ cup sugar, the cornstarch and cinnamon. Add pears and cranberries; toss gently to coat. Spoon into crust-lined pan.

3. In small bowl, mix all topping ingredients with fork until well blended. Sprinkle over filling.

4. Place tart on cookie sheet in oven. Bake 45 to 55 minutes or until crust is deep golden brown and pears are tender. Serve warm or cool.

Fresh cranberries are available October through December. The ruby-red berries can be refrigerated up to 2 months and freeze very well up to 1 year in the original plastic bag.

High Altitude (3500–6500 ft): No change.

1 Serving: Calories 290 (Calories from Fat 90); Total Fat 10g (Saturated Fat 4.5g; Trans Fat 0g); Cholesterol 10mg; Sodium 130mg; Total Carbohydrate 50g (Dietary Fiber 3g; Sugars 27g); Protein 0g % Daily Value: Vitamin A 2%; Vitamin C 4%; Calcium 0%; Iron 4% Exchanges: $1/2$ Fruit, 3 Other Carbohydrate, 2 Fat Carbohydrate Choices: 3

pumpkin tart with caramel rum-raisin sauce

Prep Time: **35 minutes**   Start to Finish: **2 hours 25 minutes**   12 servings

CRUST

1 refrigerated pie crust (from 15-oz box), softened as directed on box

FILLING

$^3/_4$ cup sugar

$^3/_4$ teaspoon ground cinnamon

$^1/_2$ teaspoon ground ginger

$^1/_8$ teaspoon ground cloves

$^1/_2$ cup milk

1 can (15 oz) pumpkin (not pumpkin pie mix)

2 eggs

SAUCE

1 cup packed brown sugar

$^1/_4$ cup whipping cream

$^1/_4$ cup dark rum*

$^1/_4$ cup dark corn syrup

$^1/_2$ cup raisins

1 Place cookie sheet in oven on middle oven rack. Heat oven to 450°F. Place pie crust in 10-inch tart pan with removable bottom as directed on box for One-Crust Filled Pie.

2 In large bowl, blend all filling ingredients. Pour into crust-lined pan.

3 Place tart on cookie sheet in oven. Bake 35 to 50 minutes or until crust is deep golden brown. Cool 1 hour.

4 In medium saucepan, mix all sauce ingredients. Cook over medium heat, stirring constantly, until mixture comes to a boil. Reduce heat to low; simmer 5 minutes, stirring constantly. Serve sauce with tart. Store in refrigerator.

*1 $^1/_2$ teaspoons rum extract plus $^1/_4$ cup water can be substituted for dark rum.

If raisins aren't your favorite, just leave them out of the sauce. This sauce is also delicious drizzled over ice cream or slices of pound cake.

High Altitude (3500–6500 ft): Bake 40 to 50 minutes.

1 Serving: Calories 290 (Calories from Fat 70); Total Fat 7g (Saturated Fat 3g; Trans Fat 0g); Cholesterol 45mg; Sodium 110mg; Total Carbohydrate 53g (Dietary Fiber 1g; Sugars 38g); Protein 2g % Daily Value: Vitamin A 110%; Vitamin C 0%; Calcium 4%; Iron 6% Exchanges: $^1/_2$ Starch, 3 Other Carbohydrate, 1 $^1/_2$ Fat Carbohydrate Choices: 3 $^1/_2$

peppermint-fudge pie

Prep Time: **25 minutes**   Start to Finish: **2 hours 10 minutes**   8 servings

CRUST

1 refrigerated pie crust (from 15-oz box), softened as directed on box

FILLING

2 cups milk

1 box (4-serving size) chocolate pudding and pie filling mix (not instant)

$1/2$ cup semisweet chocolate chips

1 package (8 oz) cream cheese, softened

$1/2$ cup powdered sugar

1 teaspoon peppermint extract

2 drops green or red food color

2 cups frozen whipped topping, thawed

Shaved chocolate, if desired

1 Heat oven to 450°F. Make pie crust as directed on box for One-Crust Baked Shell using 9-inch glass pie plate. Bake 9 to 11 minutes or until light golden brown. Cool completely, about 30 minutes.

2 Meanwhile, in medium saucepan, mix milk and pudding mix. Heat to boiling over medium heat, stirring constantly. Remove from heat. Stir in chocolate chips until melted. Place plastic wrap directly over surface of pudding. Refrigerate just until cooled, about 45 minutes.

3 In small bowl, beat cream cheese, powdered sugar, peppermint extract and food color with electric mixer on medium speed until smooth. Gradually add 1 cup of the whipped topping, beating on low speed until combined. Spread in cooled baked shell.

4 Stir cooled pudding mixture; spread over cream cheese layer. Carefully spread remaining 1 cup whipped topping over pudding layer. Garnish with shaved chocolate. Refrigerate until chilled before serving, about 1 hour. Store in refrigerator.

Lovely layers of mint green, chocolate and whipped topping make a slice of this pie worthy of any restaurant dessert tray. For a festive garnish, use small foil-wrapped three-layer rectangular chocolate mints and grate or shred over pie.

High Altitude (3500–6500 ft):
No change.

1 Serving: Calories 430 (Calories from Fat 220); Total Fat 25g (Saturated Fat 14g; Trans Fat 0g); Cholesterol 40mg; Sodium 280mg; Total Carbohydrate 47g (Dietary Fiber 1g; Sugars 27g); Protein 5g % Daily Value: Vitamin A 10%; Vitamin C 0%; Calcium 10%; Iron 4% Exchanges: 1 Starch, 2 Other Carbohydrate, 5 Fat Carbohydrate Choices: 3

tropical pineapple–cream cheese tart

Prep Time: **25 minutes**   Start to Finish: **1 hour 50 minutes**   **10 servings**

CRUST

1 refrigerated pie crust (from 15-
oz box), softened as directed
on box

1 teaspoon sugar

FILLING

1 package (8 oz) cream cheese,
softened

$^1/_4$ cup sugar

1 teaspoon coconut extract*

1 egg

TOPPING

1 can (20 oz) crushed pineapple
in syrup, well drained, $^1/_4$ cup
syrup reserved

2 teaspoons cornstarch

1 Heat oven to 450°F. Remove crust from pouch; unroll on work surface. Sprinkle with 1 teaspoon sugar; roll in lightly with rolling pin. Press crust, sugar side up, in bottom and up side of 10- or 9-inch tart pan with removable bottom. Trim edge if necessary.

2 Bake 7 to 9 minutes or until light golden brown. Remove partially baked shell from oven. Cool while making filling. Reduce oven temperature to 400°F.

3 In small bowl, beat cream cheese with electric mixer on medium speed until light and fluffy. Add $^1/_4$ cup sugar, the coconut extract and egg; beat until well blended. Pour into partially baked shell. Carefully spoon pineapple over cream cheese mixture. (Pineapple will not completely cover cream cheese.)

4 Bake 20 to 25 minutes or until filling is puffed around edge and set.

5 Meanwhile, in small saucepan, mix reserved $^1/_4$ cup pineapple syrup and the cornstarch until smooth. Cook over medium heat, stirring frequently, until glaze boils and thickens.

6 Spoon pineapple glaze over pineapple. Cool completely before serving, about 1 hour. Store in refrigerator.

*If you can't find coconut extract, substitute vanilla extract.

High Altitude (3500–6500 ft): Reserve
$^1/_3$ cup pineapple syrup. Bake filled pie at
400°F for 25 to 30 minutes.

1 Serving: Calories 240 (Calories from Fat 130); Total Fat 14g (Saturated Fat 7g; Trans Fat 0g); Cholesterol 50mg; Sodium 160mg; Total Carbohydrate 26g (Dietary Fiber 0g; Sugars 14g); Protein 3g % Daily Value: Vitamin A 8%; Vitamin C 4%; Calcium 2%; Iron 2% Exchanges: 1 Starch, 1 Other Carbohydrate, 2 $^1/_2$ Fat Carbohydrate Choices: 2

classic pecan pie

Prep Time: **15 minutes**   Start to Finish: **2 hours 10 minutes**   8 servings

CRUST

1 refrigerated pie crust (from 15-oz box), softened as directed on box

FILLING

3 eggs

1 cup sugar

1 cup corn syrup

2 tablespoons butter or margarine, melted

1 teaspoon vanilla

1 ¹/₂ cups pecan halves

1 Heat oven to 350°F. Place pie crust in 9-inch glass pie plate as directed on box for One-Crust Filled Pie.

2 In medium bowl, beat eggs slightly. Add sugar, corn syrup, butter and vanilla; stir until well blended. Stir in pecans. Pour into crust-lined pan.

3 Bake 50 to 55 minutes or until filling is set around edge and slightly soft in center. Cool completely on cooling rack. Store in refrigerator.

Classics are always in style, but if you want a little culinary adventure, bake up one of these yummy variations!

California Pecan Pie: Stir ¹/₄ cup sour cream into eggs until blended.

Kentucky Bourbon Pecan Pie: Add up to 2 tablespoons bourbon to filling.

Chocolate Pecan Pie: Reduce sugar to ¹/₃ cup. Melt four 1-ounce squares semisweet baking chocolate with the butter.

High Altitude (3500–6500 ft): No change.

1 Serving: Calories 540 (Calories from Fat 230); Total Fat 25g (Saturated Fat 6g; Trans Fat 0g); Cholesterol 90mg; Sodium 200mg; Total Carbohydrate 74g (Dietary Fiber 2g; Sugars 41g); Protein 4g % Daily Value: Vitamin A 4%; Vitamin C 0%; Calcium 2%; Iron 4% Exchanges: 1 Starch, 4 Other Carbohydrate, 5 Fat Carbohydrate Choices: 5

"gingerbread boy" cake

Prep Time: **55 minutes**   Start to Finish: **2 hours**   16 servings

CAKE

1 box (1 lb 2.25 oz) German
    chocolate cake mix with
    pudding

1 ¹/₄ cups water

¹/₂ cup vegetable oil

3 eggs

1 bag (6 oz) semisweet
    chocolate chips (1 cup)

FROSTING AND DECORATIONS

1 container (1 lb) vanilla creamy
    ready-to-spread frosting

1 container (1 lb) chocolate
    creamy ready-to-spread
    frosting

3 large red gumdrops

2 milk chocolate stars

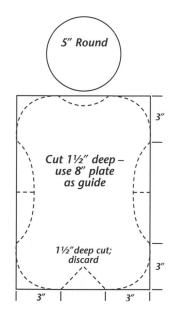

5" Round

*Cut 1½" deep –
use 8" plate
as guide*

3"

3"

*1½" deep cut;
discard*

3"

3"   3"

1 Heat oven to 350°F (if using dark or nonstick pans, heat oven to 325°F). Grease bottom of 13 × 9-inch pan with shortening; line with waxed paper. Grease waxed paper with shortening; lightly flour. Generously grease 5-inch round ovenproof bowl that holds at least 1 cup with shortening; lightly flour.

2 In large bowl, beat cake mix, water, oil and eggs with electric mixer on low speed 30 seconds or until moistened. Beat on medium speed 2 minutes, scraping bowl occasionally. Pour ¹/₂ cup batter into greased and floured bowl; pour remaining batter into pan. Sprinkle 2 tablespoons of the chocolate chips on batter in bowl; sprinkle remaining chips on batter in pan.

3 Bake bowl 17 to 22 minutes and pan 27 to 35 minutes or until cake springs back when touched lightly in center. Cool cakes 10 minutes. Invert onto cooling rack; remove waxed paper. Cool completely, about 30 minutes. To easily cut cake shapes, chill it thoroughly before cutting it in step 5. Invert onto flat serving tray or foil-covered cardboard, about 20 × 14 inches.

4 Spoon ¹/₂ cup of the vanilla frosting into resealable food-storage plastic bag. Seal bag; set aside. In medium bowl, blend remaining vanilla frosting and the chocolate frosting.

5 Using serrated knife, cut cake as shown in diagram. Spread cut edge of neck with frosting; attach round cake piece for head. Spread thin layer of frosting over all cut areas. Spread remaining frosting evenly over cake. Cut off one small corner of bag with vanilla frosting. Pipe frosting onto cake and decorate as shown in photo.

High Altitude (3500–6500 ft):
No change.

1 Serving: Calories 520 (Calories from Fat 230); Total Fat 25g (Saturated Fat 7g; Trans Fat 4.5g); Cholesterol 40mg; Sodium 420mg; Total Carbohydrate 69g (Dietary Fiber 1g; Sugars 53g); Protein 3g % Daily Value: Vitamin A 0%; Vitamin C 0%; Calcium 4%; Iron 8% Exchanges: 1 Starch, 3 ¹/₂ Other Carbohydrate, 5 Fat Carbohydrate Choices: 4 ¹/₂

santa claus cake

Prep Time: **50 minutes**   Start to Finish: **2 hours 15 minutes**   12 servings

CAKE

1 box (1 lb 2.25 oz) yellow cake
  mix with pudding

1 1/4 cups water

1/3 cup vegetable oil

3 eggs

FROSTING AND DECORATIONS

1 large marshmallow

1 container (1 lb) vanilla creamy
  ready-to-spread frosting

1/2 cup flaked coconut

1 to 2 tablespoons red sugar

1 teaspoon red edible glitter

1 large green gumdrop, halved

1 miniature marshmallow

3 strands pull-apart red licorice
  twists

Express your own "Santa-artistry" by using miniature marshmallows instead of coconut for the hat border and beard—or try something completely different.

1 Heat oven to 350°F (if using dark or nonstick pans, heat oven to 325°F). Generously grease 13 × 9-inch pan with shortening; lightly flour. In large bowl, beat cake mix, water, oil and eggs with electric mixer on low speed 30 seconds or until blended. Beat on medium speed 2 minutes, scraping bowl occasionally.

2 Bake 29 to 34 minutes or until toothpick inserted in center comes out clean. Cool 15 minutes. Carefully remove cake from pan. Cool completely.

3 Cover 22 × 12-inch piece heavy cardboard with foil. Cut and assemble cake pieces on foil-covered cardboard as shown in diagram.

4 Frost large marshmallow with vanilla frosting; dip in coconut. Set aside. Frost assembled cake with remaining vanilla frosting. Sprinkle red sugar on cake for top of hat; sprinkle red edible glitter on top of red sugar. Sprinkle coconut on cake for border of hat and beard.

5 Place large coconut-coated marshmallow on top of hat for tassel. Place gumdrop halves, sugar-side-up, on cake for eyes, mini marshmallow for nose and red licorice twists for mouth. Sprinkle red sugar on cake for cheeks.

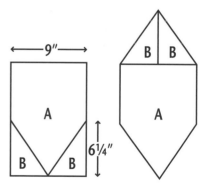

High Altitude (3500–6500 ft):
No change.

1 Serving: Calories 450 (Calories from Fat 180); Total Fat 20g (Saturated Fat 6g; Trans Fat 4g); Cholesterol 55mg; Sodium 400mg; Total Carbohydrate 65g (Dietary Fiber 0g; Sugars 46g); Protein 3g % Daily Value: Vitamin A 0%; Vitamin C 0%; Calcium 6%; Iron 6% Exchanges: 1/2 Starch, 4 Other Carbohydrate, 4 Fat Carbohydrate Choices: 4

chocolate-cherry truffle cake

Prep Time: **25 minutes**   Start to Finish: **2 hours 30 minutes**   12 servings

FILLING
1 cup semisweet chocolate chips
  (from 12-oz bag)
$^2/_3$ cup sweetened condensed
  milk (from 14-oz can)
$^1/_4$ teaspoon almond extract

CAKE
1 box (1 lb 2.25 oz) chocolate
  fudge cake mix with pudding
1 cup water
$^1/_2$ cup vegetable oil
$^1/_2$ teaspoon almond extract
4 eggs
1 box (3.9 oz) chocolate instant
  pudding and pie filling mix
1 jar (10 oz) maraschino
  cherries, drained on paper
  towel, chopped ($^3/_4$ cup)

GLAZE AND GARNISH
Remaining sweetened condensed
  milk (from 14-oz can)
$^3/_4$ cup semisweet chocolate
  chips (from 12-oz bag)
2 tablespoons corn syrup
1 teaspoon milk, if needed
Maraschino cherries with stems,
  drained on paper towel,
  if desired

1 Heat oven to 350°F. Grease 12-cup fluted tube (bundt cake) pan with shortening; lightly flour. In medium microwavable bowl, microwave all filling ingredients on High 25 to 35 seconds, stirring every 15 seconds, until melted and smooth; set aside.

2 In large bowl, beat cake mix, water, oil, $^1/_2$ teaspoon almond extract, the eggs and pudding mix with electric mixer on low speed about 1 minute, scraping bowl constantly. With rubber spatula, fold in chopped cherries. Spoon batter into pan; spread evenly. Carefully spoon filling in ring over batter (do not let filling touch side of pan).

3 Bake 45 to 50 minutes or until toothpick inserted 1 inch from inside edge of pan comes out clean, top of cake feels firm to the touch and cake pulls away slightly from side of pan. Cool 15 minutes.

4 Place heatproof serving plate over pan; turn plate and pan over. Remove pan. Cool cake completely, about 1 hour.

5 In 1-quart saucepan, heat all glaze ingredients except milk over medium-low heat, stirring occasionally, until chocolate is melted and mixture is smooth. Stir in up to 1 teaspoon milk if necessary for desired glaze consistency. Pour glaze over cake, allowing some to drizzle down sides.

6 Decorate top of cake with maraschino cherries. Store loosely covered in refrigerator.

High Altitude (3500–6500 ft):
Heat oven to 375°F.

1 Serving: Calories 580 (Calories from Fat 220); Total Fat 24g (Saturated Fat 9g; Trans Fat 0.5g); Cholesterol 80mg; Sodium 530mg; Total Carbohydrate 83g (Dietary Fiber 3g; Sugars 63g); Protein 8g % Daily Value: Vitamin A 4%; Vitamin C 0%; Calcium 15%; Iron 15% Exchanges: 1 Starch, 4 $^1/_2$ Other Carbohydrate, $^1/_2$ High-Fat Meat, 4 Fat Carbohydrate Choices: 5 $^1/_2$

cranberry-orange pound cake

Prep Time: **15 minutes**   Start to Finish: **1 hour 45 minutes**   16 servings

CAKE

2 ³/₄ cups sugar

1 ¹/₂ cups butter or margarine, softened

1 teaspoon vanilla

1 teaspoon grated orange peel

6 eggs

3 cups all-purpose flour

1 teaspoon baking powder

¹/₂ teaspoon salt

1 container (8 oz) sour cream

1 ¹/₂ cups chopped fresh or frozen cranberries (do not thaw)

BUTTER RUM SAUCE

1 cup sugar

1 tablespoon all-purpose flour

¹/₂ cup half-and-half

¹/₂ cup butter

4 teaspoons light rum or ¹/₄ teaspoon rum extract

1 Heat oven to 350°F. Generously grease 12-cup fluted tube (bundt cake) pan with shortening; lightly flour. In large bowl, beat 2 ³/₄ cups sugar and 1 ¹/₂ cups butter until light and fluffy. Add vanilla and orange peel; blend well. Beat in 1 egg at a time until well blended.

2 In medium bowl, mix 3 cups flour, the baking powder and salt. Add to butter mixture alternately with sour cream, beating well after each addition. Gently stir in cranberries. Pour and spread batter into pan.

3 Bake 65 to 75 minutes or until toothpick inserted in center comes out clean. Cool 15 minutes. Remove from pan.

4 Meanwhile, in small saucepan, combine 1 cup sugar and 1 tablespoon flour. Stir in half-and-half and ¹/₂ cup butter. Cook over medium heat, stirring constantly, until bubbly and thickened. Remove from heat; stir in rum. Serve warm sauce over cake.

A classic American duo, cranberry and orange taste especially good at holiday time. The cake and sauce can be made up to 5 days ahead—tightly cover each and store in refrigerator. Let cake come to room temperature, and reheat sauce briefly before serving.

High Altitude (3500–6500 ft): Decrease sugar in cake to 2 ¹/₂ cups.

1 Serving: Calories 550 (Calories from Fat 260); Total Fat 29g (Saturated Fat 17g; Trans Fat 1.5g); Cholesterol 155mg; Sodium 300mg; Total Carbohydrate 68g (Dietary Fiber 1g; Sugars 48g); Protein 6g % Daily Value: Vitamin A 20%; Vitamin C 0%; Calcium 6%; Iron 8% Exchanges: 1 ¹/₂ Starch, 3 Other Carbohydrate, 5 ¹/₂ Fat Carbohydrate Choices: 4 ¹/₂

tree-shaped brownie torte

Prep Time: **40 minutes**   Start to Finish: **2 hours 10 minutes**   18 servings

BROWNIES

1 box (1 lb 3.8 oz) fudge brownie
  mix

$^1/_2$ cup vegetable oil

$^1/_4$ cup water

2 eggs

GLAZE

$^1/_2$ cup whipping cream

1 bag (6 oz) semisweet
  chocolate chips (1 cup)

FROSTING

2 cups powdered sugar

$^1/_3$ cup butter or margarine,
  softened

$^1/_2$ teaspoon vanilla

1 to 3 tablespoons milk

DECORATIONS

1 (4-oz) white chocolate baking
  bar, grated

1 chocolate-covered candy bar,
  cut in half

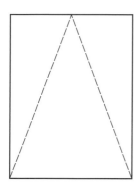

High Altitude (3500–6500 ft): Follow High Altitude
directions on brownie mix box for 13 × 9-inch pan.

1 Heat oven to 350°F. Line 13 × 9-inch pan with foil, extending foil over sides of pan; grease foil with shortening. In medium bowl, stir brownie mix, oil, water and eggs with spoon until well blended. Spread in pan.

2 Bake 28 to 30 minutes or until set. DO NOT OVERBAKE. Cool completely, about 30 minutes. Freeze brownies 30 minutes.

3 Meanwhile, in small saucepan, heat whipping cream to boiling. Remove from heat. Stir in chocolate chips until melted. Let stand about 30 minutes or until spreadable. In small bowl, blend all frosting ingredients, adding enough milk for desired spreading consistency.

4 Using foil, lift brownies from pan; place on cutting board. To cut tree shape from brownies, start at center of 1 short side and make 2 diagonal cuts to corners of opposite short side, forming a triangular piece in center. (See diagram.)

5 Place 2 side pieces together on foil-lined serving tray (or piece of heavy cardboard) to form tree shape. Spread with frosting. Top with whole tree shape. Trim if necessary to line up edges.

6 Spread glaze evenly over sides and top of brownie torte. Sprinkle top with grated white chocolate to form garland. Place candy bar half at base of tree for trunk. Let stand 15 minutes or until set.

Not all graters are alike and now there are many types available with holes of varying sizes and shapes. A grater with larger holes will give you bigger pieces of white chocolate, just like you see in the picture of this showpiece dessert.

1 Serving: Calories 390 (Calories from Fat 170); Total Fat 19g (Saturated Fat 8g; Trans Fat 1g); Cholesterol 40mg; Sodium 160mg; Total Carbohydrate 52g (Dietary Fiber 0g; Sugars 43g); Protein 3g % Daily Value: Vitamin A 4%; Vitamin C 0%; Calcium 6%; Iron 6% Exchanges: 1 Starch, 2 $^1/_2$ Other Carbohydrate, 3 $^1/_2$ Fat Carbohydrate Choices: 3 $^1/_2$

creamy cappuccino cheesecake

Prep Time: **55 minutes**   Start to Finish: **6 hours 25 minutes**   12 servings

CRUST

1 1/2 cups chocolate cookie
    crumbs

1/4 cup sugar

1/4 cup butter or margarine,
    melted

FILLING

2 tablespoons instant coffee
    granules or crystals

1 tablespoon hot water

1 teaspoon vanilla

3 packages (8 oz each) cream
    cheese, softened

1 cup sugar

1/2 teaspoon ground cinnamon

4 eggs

TOPPING

1 1/2 cups sour cream

3 tablespoons sugar

Chocolate-covered coffee beans,
    if desired

Unsweetened baking cocoa, if
    desired

1 Heat oven to 350°F. In small bowl, mix cookie crumbs, 1/4 cup sugar and the butter. Press mixture in bottom and 1 1/2 inches up side of ungreased 10-inch springform pan. Bake 10 minutes or until set. Cool 20 minutes.

2 Meanwhile, in small bowl, mix coffee granules, water and vanilla; set aside. In large bowl, beat cream cheese with electric mixer on medium speed until light and fluffy. Add 1 cup sugar; beat until very soft and creamy. Beat in cinnamon. Beat in 1 egg at a time just until well blended; do not overbeat. Add coffee mixture; mix well. Pour into cooled baked crust.

3 Bake 45 to 50 minutes or until set.

4 Meanwhile, in small bowl, blend sour cream and 3 tablespoons sugar. Spread sour cream mixture evenly over top of cheesecake; bake 10 to 15 minutes longer or until sour cream is set. Cool on cooling rack 1 1/2 hours. Refrigerate before serving, at least 3 hours or overnight. Garnish with chocolate-covered coffee beans. Sprinkle lightly with cocoa. Store in refrigerator.

High Altitude (3500–6500 ft):
No change.

1 Serving: Calories 480 (Calories from Fat 300); Total Fat 33g (Saturated Fat 19g; Trans Fat 1.5g); Cholesterol 160mg; Sodium 310mg; Total Carbohydrate 37g (Dietary Fiber 0g; Sugars 30g); Protein 8g % Daily Value: Vitamin A 25%; Vitamin C 0%; Calcium 8%; Iron 8% Exchanges: 1/2 Starch, 2 Other Carbohydrate, 1 High-Fat Meat, 5 Fat Carbohydrate Choices: 2 1/2

chocolate bread pudding with cherry-raspberry sauce

Prep Time: **30 minutes** | Start to Finish: **1 hour 10 minutes** | 20 servings

BREAD PUDDING

1 bag (6 oz) semisweet
   chocolate chips (1 cup)

1 cup whipping cream

$^2/_3$ cup packed brown sugar

5 eggs, separated

$^1/_2$ cup butter or margarine, cut
   into pieces

1 teaspoon vanilla

4 cups soft bread cubes

CHERRY-RASPBERRY SAUCE

2 tablespoons granulated sugar

4 teaspoons cornstarch

1 can (16 oz) pitted dark sweet
   cherries in syrup, drained,
   liquid reserved

1 box (10 oz) frozen raspberries
   in syrup, thawed, drained,
   liquid reserved

1 Heat oven to 350°F. Grease 12 × 8-inch (2-quart) glass baking dish with shortening. In large saucepan, heat chocolate chips and whipping cream over medium-low heat, stirring occasionally, until chips are melted. Stir in $^1/_3$ cup of the brown sugar. Beat in 1 egg yolk at a time until well blended. Continue cooking until slightly thickened. Add butter and vanilla; stir until smooth. Remove from heat; stir in bread cubes.

2 In large bowl, beat egg whites with electric mixer on medium speed until soft peaks form. Gradually add remaining $^1/_3$ cup brown sugar, beating on highest speed until stiff peaks form. Fold egg whites into chocolate mixture. Pour into baking dish; place baking dish on 15 × 10 × 1-inch pan. Place pan in oven; pour boiling water into 15 × 10 × 1-inch pan until water is $^1/_2$ to $^3/_4$ inch deep. Bake 35 to 40 minutes or until center is set.

3 In medium saucepan, mix granulated sugar and cornstarch. Gradually stir in reserved liquids from fruits. Cook over medium-high heat, stirring constantly, until mixture boils and thickens. Cool slightly; stir in fruit. Serve over warm bread pudding. Store any remaining bread pudding and sauce in refrigerator.

To really make this a "to-die-for" fantasy dessert, spoon generous dollops of whipped cream on each serving and then drizzle with warm hot fudge sauce or chocolate sauce. Go all out by topping it off with a chocolate-covered long-stemmed cherry!

High Altitude (3500–6500 ft):
No change.

1 Serving: Calories 230 (Calories from Fat 110); Total Fat 12g (Saturated Fat 7g; Trans Fat 0g); Cholesterol 80mg; Sodium 105mg; Total Carbohydrate 27g (Dietary Fiber 2g; Sugars 21g); Protein 3g % Daily Value: Vitamin A 8%; Vitamin C 2%; Calcium 4%; Iron 6% Exchanges: 1 Starch, 1 Other Carbohydrate, 2 Fat Carbohydrate Choices: 2

eggnog crème brûlée

Prep Time: **20 minutes**   Start to Finish: **4 hours 25 minutes**   8 servings

3 cups whipping cream

5 egg yolks

2 eggs

$^1/_2$ cup granulated sugar

2 tablespoons dark rum

1 tablespoon brandy

1 teaspoon vanilla*

$^1/_2$ teaspoon ground nutmeg

Boiling water

$^1/_2$ cup packed brown sugar

Ceramic ramekins

are small, individual-size baking dishes; look for them at large discount stores, department stores or kitchen specialty shops.

1 Heat oven to 325°F. Place eight 6-ounce ceramic ramekins in 15 × 10 × 1-inch pan. In medium saucepan, heat whipping cream just to a simmer. Remove from heat.

2 In medium bowl, beat egg yolks and eggs. Stir in granulated sugar until combined. With wire whisk, stir in hot whipping cream until well blended. Stir in rum, brandy, vanilla and nutmeg. Pour mixture into ramekins.

3 Place pan in oven; pour boiling water into pan, being careful not to splash water into ramekins, until water is $^1/_2$ to $^3/_4$ inch deep.

4 Bake 30 to 35 minutes or until centers are just set. Carefully transfer ramekins to cooling rack using tongs or grasping tops of ramekins with pot holder. Cool 30 minutes. Refrigerate at least 3 hours or overnight.

5 Before serving, heat oven control to broil. Place ramekins in 15 × 10 × 1-inch pan; top each with 1 tablespoon brown sugar. Broil 5 to 6 inches from heat 1 to 2 minutes or until sugar is melted and forms a glaze. (Watch closely.) Store in refrigerator.

*To make classic Crème Brûlée, omit the rum, brandy and nutmeg; increase vanilla to 1 $^1/_2$ teaspoons.

High Altitude (3500–6500 ft): No change.

1 Serving: Calories 430 (Calories from Fat 290); Total Fat 32g (Saturated Fat 19g; Trans Fat 1g); Cholesterol 280mg; Sodium 55mg; Total Carbohydrate 29g (Dietary Fiber 0g; Sugars 28g); Protein 5g % Daily Value: Vitamin A 25%; Vitamin C 0%; Calcium 10%; Iron 4% Exchanges: 2 Other Carbohydrate, $^1/_2$ Medium-Fat Meat, 6 Fat Carbohydrate Choices: 2

cherry-cheese crescent braid

Prep Time: **20 minutes**	Start to Finish: **55 minutes**	8 servings

BRAID

1 can (8 oz) refrigerated crescent
   dinner rolls

$^1/_2$ cup pineapple cream cheese
   spread (from 8-oz container)

2 tablespoons granulated sugar

1 egg, separated

$^1/_2$ cup chopped candied red
   cherries

1 tablespoon water

1 teaspoon granulated sugar

GLAZE

$^1/_3$ cup powdered sugar

$^1/_4$ teaspoon almond extract

1 to 2 teaspoons milk

Red candied cherries, if desired

1 Heat oven to 375°F. Spray cookie sheet with cooking spray. Unroll dough onto cookie sheet, forming 13 × 7-inch rectangle. Firmly press perforations to seal.

2 In medium bowl, beat cream cheese and 2 tablespoons granulated sugar. Beat in egg yolk. Stir in chopped cherries. Spoon lengthwise down center of dough rectangle in 2 $^1/_2$-inch-wide strip. Cut 1-inch-wide strips on each side of cream cheese filling to within $^1/_2$ inch of filling. Fold strips at an angle across filling mixture, alternating from side to side. (See diagram.)

3 In small bowl, beat egg white and water. Brush egg white mixture over dough. (Discard any remaining egg white mixture.) Sprinkle with 1 teaspoon granulated sugar.

4 Bake 15 to 20 minutes or until deep golden brown. Immediately remove from cookie sheet; place on serving tray. Cool 5 minutes.

5 In small bowl, mix powdered sugar, almond extract and enough milk for desired glaze consistency. Drizzle glaze over warm braid. Garnish with candied cherries. Cool 15 minutes before slicing. Serve warm. Store in refrigerator.

For an elegant presentation, garnish the platter with stemmed maraschino cherries.

High Altitude (3500–6500 ft): Bake 15 to 18 minutes.

1 Serving: Calories 230 (Calories from Fat 100); Total Fat 11g (Saturated Fat 5g; Trans Fat 1.5g); Cholesterol 40mg; Sodium 340mg; Total Carbohydrate 29g (Dietary Fiber 0g; Sugars 18g); Protein 4g % Daily Value: Vitamin A 4%; Vitamin C 0%; Calcium 2%; Iron 4% Exchanges: 1 Starch, 1 Other Carbohydrate, 2 Fat Carbohydrate Choices: 2

cranberry cream cheese swirl loaf

Prep Time: **20 minutes**   Start to Finish: **2 hours 50 minutes**   1 loaf (16 slices)

2 packages (3 oz each) cream
  cheese, softened

1 egg

2 cups all-purpose flour

1 cup sugar

1 $^1/_2$ teaspoons baking powder

$^1/_2$ teaspoon baking soda

$^1/_2$ teaspoon salt

$^3/_4$ cup apple juice

$^1/_4$ cup butter or margarine,
  melted

1 egg, beaten

1 $^1/_2$ cups coarsely chopped
  fresh cranberries

$^1/_2$ cup chopped nuts

1 Heat oven to 350°F. Grease bottom only of 9 × 5-inch loaf pan with shortening; lightly flour. In small bowl, beat cream cheese until light and fluffy. Add 1 egg; blend well. Set aside.

2 In large bowl, mix flour, sugar, baking powder, baking soda and salt. Stir in apple juice, butter and beaten egg until well blended. Fold in cranberries and nuts. Spoon half of batter into pan. Spoon cream cheese mixture evenly over batter. Top with remaining batter.

3 Bake 65 to 75 minutes or until top springs back when touched lightly in center. Cool 15 minutes; remove from pan. Cool completely, about 1 hour. Wrap tightly and store in refrigerator.

Show off this bread's assets! Fan slices on a serving tray to reveal the cream cheese layer in the center. How about Orange-Cranberry Cream Cheese Swirl Loaf? Substitute orange juice for the apple juice and add 1 teaspoon grated orange peel to the batter in step 2.

High Altitude (3500–6500 ft): Heat oven to 375°F. Increase flour to 2 cups plus 3 tablespoons; decrease sugar to $^1/_2$ cup. Bake 55 to 65 minutes.

1 Slice: Calories 220 (Calories from Fat 90); Total Fat 10g (Saturated Fat 4.5g; Trans Fat 0g); Cholesterol 45mg; Sodium 220mg; Total Carbohydrate 28g (Dietary Fiber 1g; Sugars 14g); Protein 4g % Daily Value: Vitamin A 6%; Vitamin C 0%; Calcium 4%; Iron 6% Exchanges: $^1/_2$ Starch, 1 $^1/_2$ Other Carbohydrate, 2 Fat Carbohydrate Choices: 2

mocha streusel coffee cake

| Prep Time: **25 minutes** | Start to Finish: **2 hours 30 minutes** | 12 servings |

STREUSEL

1/3 cup packed brown sugar

2 tablespoons all-purpose flour

1 tablespoon instant coffee
   granules or crystals

4 oz semisweet baking
   chocolate, chopped

1/2 cup pecan pieces

COFFEE CAKE

1 cup granulated sugar

1 cup butter or margarine,
   softened

3 eggs

1/2 teaspoon almond extract

2 3/4 cups all-purpose flour

2 teaspoons baking powder

1 teaspoon ground cinnamon

1/4 teaspoon baking soda

1/4 teaspoon salt

1 container (8 oz) plain yogurt

1 Heat oven to 350°F. Spray angel food (tube cake) pan with cooking spray. In food processor bowl with metal blade, place brown sugar, 2 tablespoons flour and the instant coffee. Cover; process with on-and-off pulses until mixed. Add chocolate; pulse to finely chop. Add pecans; pulse to chop. Set aside.

2 In large bowl, beat granulated sugar and butter with electric mixer on medium speed until fluffy. Beat in 1 egg at a time until well blended. Add almond extract; mix well.

3 In small bowl, mix 2 3/4 cups flour, the baking powder, cinnamon, baking soda and salt. Add half of flour mixture to sugar-egg mixture; beat with electric mixer on low speed just until combined. Add yogurt; blend well. Add remaining flour mixture; mix well.

4 Spoon half of batter into pan, spreading evenly. Sprinkle with half of streusel mixture. Top with remaining batter and remaining streusel mixture.

5 Bake 55 to 65 minutes or until toothpick inserted in center comes out clean. Cool upright in pan on cooling rack 1 hour. Remove cake from pan. Serve warm or cool.

Make a date to meet for coffee or tea with friends, and bring along this warm coffee cake—what a nice surprise. Remember to take a plastic knife and some paper plates or napkins, too.

High Altitude (3500–6500 ft):
Increase flour in coffee cake to 3 cups.

1 Serving: Calories 450 (Calories from Fat 210); Total Fat 23g (Saturated Fat 12g; Trans Fat 1g); Cholesterol 95mg; Sodium 300mg; Total Carbohydrate 54g (Dietary Fiber 2g; Sugars 29g); Protein 7g % Daily Value: Vitamin A 10%; Vitamin C 0%; Calcium 10%; Iron 15% Exchanges: 2 Starch, 1 1/2 Other Carbohydrate, 4 1/2 Fat Carbohydrate Choices: 3 1/2

christmas tree coffee cake

Prep Time: **15 minutes**	Start to Finish: **35 minutes**	8 servings

BREAD

1 can (8 oz) refrigerated crescent
  dinner rolls

2 teaspoons granulated sugar

1 teaspoon grated orange peel

GLAZE

$1/4$ cup powdered sugar

1 to 2 teaspoons orange juice

4 candied red cherries, halved

4 candied green cherries, halved

1 Heat oven to 375°F. Unroll dough into 2 long rectangles; firmly press perforations to seal. Cut each rectangle lengthwise into 4 strips. Twist each dough strip several times.

2 On ungreased cookie sheet, form tree shape by starting at top of tree. Zigzag twisted strips of dough back and forth across cookie sheet, touching previous strip and making tree wider toward bottom, adding strips as each is finished. End with curl of dough at center of bottom to form trunk. Tree will be about 8 inches from tip to trunk.

3 In small bowl, mix granulated sugar and orange peel. Sprinkle over dough.

4 Bake 12 to 16 minutes or until golden brown. Immediately remove from cookie sheet; place on serving tray.

5 In small bowl, beat powdered sugar and orange juice until smooth and thin enough to drizzle. Drizzle glaze over bread. Garnish with cherries. Serve warm.

Don't like candied cherries? Try fresh raspberries, strawberry slices, dried cranberries or very well-drained maraschino cherries instead. While you're at it, make an extra coffee cake for a friend!

High Altitude (3500–6500 ft):
No change.

1 Serving: Calories 130 (Calories from Fat 50); Total Fat 6g (Saturated Fat 2g; Trans Fat 1.5g); Cholesterol 0mg; Sodium 220mg; Total Carbohydrate 18g (Dietary Fiber 0g; Sugars 8g); Protein 2g % Daily Value: Vitamin A 0%; Vitamin C 0%; Calcium 0%; Iron 4% Exchanges: 1 Starch, 1 Fat Carbohydrate Choices: 1

cherry pistachio scones

Prep Time: **35 minutes**   Start to Finish: **1 hour 10 minutes**   12 scones

2 cups all-purpose flour

2 tablespoons sugar

3 teaspoons baking powder

$3/4$ teaspoon ground cinnamon

$1/2$ cup butter or margarine

$3/4$ cup chopped drained
   maraschino cherries

$1/2$ cup chopped shelled
   pistachio nuts

$1/2$ cup milk

1 egg, separated

4 teaspoons coarse white
   sparkling sugar or granulated
   sugar

1 Heat oven to 375°F. Line cookie sheet with parchment paper or lightly grease cookie sheet with shortening. In large bowl, mix flour, 2 tablespoons sugar, the baking powder and cinnamon. With pastry blender or fork, cut in butter until mixture resembles coarse crumbs. Stir in cherries and pistachios.

2 In small bowl, blend milk and egg yolk. Add to flour mixture. Stir just until dry ingredients are moistened.

3 On lightly floured surface, gently knead dough several times. Divide dough in half; place on cookie sheet. Pat each half into 6-inch round. Cut each round into 6 wedges; do not separate. In small bowl, beat egg white. Brush top of each round with egg white; sprinkle with coarse sugar.

4 Bake 17 to 22 minutes or until golden brown. Cool 10 minutes before serving.

Pistachio nuts are available in their natural tan shell, or in a dyed red shell. Don't use the red pistachios for this recipe because the red dye bleeds into the dough.

High Altitude (3500–6500 ft):
No change.

1 Scone: Calories 220 (Calories from Fat 100); Total Fat 11g (Saturated Fat 5g; Trans Fat 0g); Cholesterol 40mg; Sodium 190mg; Total Carbohydrate 26g (Dietary Fiber 2g; Sugars 8g); Protein 4g % Daily Value: Vitamin A 6%; Vitamin C 0%; Calcium 10%; Iron 8% Exchanges: $1/2$ Starch, 1 $1/2$ Other Carbohydrate, 2 Fat Carbohydrate Choices: 2

caramel sticky buns

extra easy

| Prep Time: **15 minutes** | Start to Finish: **35 minutes** | 12 rolls |

TOPPING

¹/₄ cup butter or margarine, melted

¹/₄ cup packed brown sugar

2 tablespoons light corn syrup

¹/₄ cup chopped pecans

BUNS

1 tablespoon granulated sugar

¹/₂ teaspoon ground cinnamon

1 can (12 oz) refrigerated flaky biscuits

1 Heat oven to 375°F. Grease 12 regular-size muffin cups with shortening. In small bowl, mix all topping ingredients. Spoon scant tablespoon topping into each muffin cup.

2 In plastic bag, mix sugar and cinnamon. Separate dough into 10 biscuits. Cut each biscuit into 6 pieces. Shake pieces in sugar mixture. Place 5 pieces of dough in each muffin cup.

3 Place pan on foil or cookie sheet to guard against spills. Bake 15 to 20 minutes or until golden brown. Cool 1 minute. Invert onto waxed paper. Serve warm.

Refrigerated biscuits are the key to these very quick and easy, ooey-gooey buns. For a deeper, richer flavor, substitute dark corn syrup for the light version.

High Altitude (3500–6500 ft):
No change.

1 Roll: Calories 170 (Calories from Fat 80); Total Fat 9g (Saturated Fat 3.5g; Trans Fat 1.5g); Cholesterol 10mg; Sodium 330mg; Total Carbohydrate 20g (Dietary Fiber 0g; Sugars 9g); Protein 2g % Daily Value: Vitamin A 2%; Vitamin C 0%; Calcium 0%; Iron 4% Exchanges: 1 ¹/₂ Other Carbohydrate, 2 Fat Carbohydrate Choices: 1

pesto angel wing rolls

Prep Time: **5 minutes**	Start to Finish: **25 minutes**	8 rolls

1/4 cup 1/3-less-fat cream cheese
(Neufchâtel), softened

2 tablespoons basil pesto

1 can (11 oz) refrigerated
original breadsticks

1 Heat oven to 350°F. In small bowl, mix cream cheese and pesto.

2 Remove dough from can. Unroll but do not separate dough. Spread cream cheese mixture evenly over dough. Reroll dough; seal well. Cut into 8 rolls at perforations. Place on ungreased cookie sheet. With kitchen scissors or knife, make 1-inch-long cut (almost to the center) on two opposite sides of each roll.

3 Bake 16 to 20 minutes or until golden brown.

Look like a professional baker! To create shiny golden tops, beat 1 egg white with 1 tablespoon water and brush on tops of rolls before baking.

High Altitude (3500–6500 ft):
No change.

1 Roll: Calories 140 (Calories from Fat 50); Total Fat 6g (Saturated Fat 2g; Trans Fat 0g); Cholesterol 5mg; Sodium 340mg; Total Carbohydrate 19g (Dietary Fiber 0g; Sugars 2g); Protein 4g % Daily Value: Vitamin A 2%; Vitamin C 0%; Calcium 0%; Iron 6% Exchanges: 1 Starch, 1 Fat Carbohydrate Choices: 1

quick and easy onion rolls

Prep Time: **20 minutes**   Start to Finish: **40 minutes**   12 rolls

$^1/_4$ cup finely chopped onion

3 tablespoons chopped pine nuts

3 tablespoons finely chopped
   sun-dried tomatoes in oil,
   drained, 1 tablespoon oil
   reserved

1 tablespoon poppy seed

1 can (11 oz) refrigerated
   original breadsticks

$^1/_4$ cup shredded fresh Parmesan
   cheese (1 oz)

1 Heat oven to 375°F. Grease cookie sheet with shortening. In small skillet, cook and stir onion, pine nuts and tomatoes over medium heat 1 to 2 minutes or until onion is tender and nuts are toasted. Remove from heat. Stir in poppy seed.

2 Unroll dough; separate into 2 sections (6 breadsticks each). Spread onion mixture over dough. Reroll dough sections; pinch edges to seal. Cut each section into 6 rolls. Place rolls cut side up on cookie sheet. Brush with reserved 1 tablespoon tomato oil. Sprinkle with cheese.

3 Bake 13 to 17 minutes or until golden brown. Serve warm.

Pine nuts, also called piñon, pignoli and pignolia are the high-fat nuts found inside the pine cone of several types of pine tree. They have a very tender texture and very mild flavor; if you can't find them, use slivered almonds instead.

High Altitude (3500–6500 ft):
No change.

1 Roll: Calories 110 (Calories from Fat 45); Total Fat 5g (Saturated Fat 1g; Trans Fat 0g); Cholesterol 0mg; Sodium 230mg; Total Carbohydrate 14g (Dietary Fiber 0g; Sugars 2g); Protein 3g % Daily Value: Vitamin A 0%; Vitamin C 0%; Calcium 4%; Iron 6% Exchanges: 1 Starch, 1 Fat Carbohydrate Choices: 1

holiday biscuit cutouts

| Prep Time: **15 minutes** | Start to Finish: **35 minutes** | 12 biscuits |

2 ¼ cups all-purpose flour

2 teaspoons baking powder

½ teaspoon baking soda

¼ teaspoon salt

½ lb bulk pork sausage, cooked, crumbled and well drained

2 tablespoons butter or margarine

¼ cup finely chopped pecans

¾ to 1 cup buttermilk*

2 tablespoons milk

1 Heat oven to 400°F. Grease cookie sheet with shortening. In large bowl, mix flour, baking powder, baking soda and salt. Using fork or pastry blender, cut in sausage, butter and pecans until mixture resembles fine crumbs. Stir in buttermilk, adding enough to form soft dough.

2 Turn dough out onto well-floured surface; knead dough 5 to 6 times. On lightly floured surface, roll out dough to ½-inch thickness. Cut with floured 3-inch holiday cookie cutter or 3-inch biscuit cutter. Place biscuits 2 inches apart on cookie sheet; brush with milk.

3 Bake 15 to 20 minutes or until light golden brown. Immediately remove from cookie sheet. Cool slightly on cooling rack.

*To substitute for buttermilk, use 2 ¼ to 3 teaspoons vinegar or lemon juice plus milk to make ¾ to 1 cup.

Mix it up by using different holiday cookie cutter shapes to cut out these scrumptious biscuits. Serve the biscuits as a side with your favorite entrée or whip up a packet of country gravy mix to pour over the biscuits for a hearty breakfast.

High Altitude (3500–6500 ft): No change.

1 Biscuit: Calories 160 (Calories from Fat 60); Total Fat 7g (Saturated Fat 2.5g; Trans Fat 0g); Cholesterol 15mg; Sodium 280mg; Total Carbohydrate 19g (Dietary Fiber 0g; Sugars 1g); Protein 5g % Daily Value: Vitamin A 0%; Vitamin C 0%; Calcium 8%; Iron 8% Exchanges: ½ Starch, 1 Other Carbohydrate, ½ High-Fat Meat, ½ Fat Carbohydrate Choices: 1

spinach dip crescent wreath

| Prep Time: **30 minutes** | Start to Finish: **1 hour 20 minutes** | 20 servings |

2 cans (8 oz each) refrigerated crescent dinner rolls

1 ¹/₂ cups spinach dip

¹/₄ cup chopped red bell pepper

2 tablespoons chopped green onions (2 medium)

1 tablespoon chopped fresh parsley

Green bell pepper, cut into holly leaf shapes

Small cherry tomatoes

This appetizer is the perfect answer to the question, "What can I bring?" The cheery ring-shape looks like an evergreen wreath dotted with holly leaves and berries.

1 Heat oven to 375°F. Invert 10-ounce custard cup* on center of ungreased large cookie sheet.

2 Remove dough from 1 can, keeping dough in 1 piece; DO NOT UNROLL. (Keep remaining can of dough in refrigerator.) With hands, roll dough in one direction to form 12-inch log. Cut log into 20 slices. Arrange 16 slices, slightly overlapping, around custard cup on cookie sheet.

3 Repeat with second can of dough, cutting log into 20 slices. Arrange slices from second can and remaining 4 slices from first can (total of 24 slices), slightly overlapping each other, next to but not overlapping first ring. Remove custard cup.

4 Bake 14 to 18 minutes or until light golden brown. Gently loosen wreath from cookie sheet; carefully slide onto cooling rack. Cool completely, about 30 minutes.

5 Place cooled wreath on serving tray or platter. Spread spinach dip over wreath. Sprinkle with red bell pepper, onions and parsley. Decorate with bell pepper "holly leaves" and cherry tomato "berries." Serve immediately, or cover and refrigerate up to 2 hours before serving.

*A 4 ¹/₂-inch round ovenproof bowl (inverted), empty can, or ball of crumpled foil can be used instead of a 10-ounce custard cup.

High Altitude (3500–6500 ft): No change.

1 Serving: Calories 120 (Calories from Fat 70); Total Fat 8g (Saturated Fat 2.5g; Trans Fat 1g); Cholesterol 0mg; Sodium 280mg; Total Carbohydrate 11g (Dietary Fiber 0g; Sugars 3g); Protein 2g % Daily Value: Vitamin A 15%; Vitamin C 6%; Calcium 0%; Iron 4% Exchanges: ¹/₂ Starch, ¹/₂ Other Carbohydrate, 1 ¹/₂ Fat Carbohydrate Choices: 1

savory crab cheesecake

Prep Time: **20 minutes**   Start to Finish: **4 hours 30 minutes**   20 servings (¹/₄ cup cheesecake and 5 crackers each)

CRUST

¹/₂ cup Italian style dry bread crumbs

¹/₄ cup shredded Parmesan cheese (1 oz)

2 tablespoons butter, melted

FILLING

20 oz cream cheese, softened

2 tablespoons finely chopped green onions (2 medium)

1 ¹/₂ teaspoons Creole seasoning

1 teaspoon sugar

¹/₂ teaspoon ground mustard

Dash ground red pepper

¹/₂ cup whipping cream

1 tablespoon cocktail sauce

1 teaspoon Worcestershire sauce

¹/₂ teaspoon red pepper sauce

4 eggs

1 can (6 oz) crabmeat, drained

GARNISH AND SERVE WITH

Fresh sage leaves

Cocktail sauce, if desired

Assorted crackers, if desired

1 Heat oven to 350°F. In small bowl, mix all crust ingredients. Press mixture in bottom of ungreased 8- or 9-inch springform pan. Bake 5 to 9 minutes or until light golden brown.

2 Meanwhile, in large bowl, beat all filling ingredients except eggs and crabmeat with electric mixer on medium speed until well blended. Beat in 1 egg at a time until well blended. Stir in crabmeat. Pour filling over partially baked crust.

3 Bake 60 to 70 minutes longer for 8-inch pan; 40 to 50 minutes for 9-inch pan or until filling is set. Cool 30 minutes.

4 With small metal spatula or knife, loosen edge of cheesecake. Cool 30 minutes longer. Refrigerate before serving, at least 2 hours.

5 To serve, remove side of pan; place cheesecake on serving platter. Arrange sage around outer edge. Serve with additional cocktail sauce and crackers.

Wow! This appetizer cheesecake is so impressive and utterly delicious. If you have trouble finding the Creole seasoning, go ahead and use Cajun seasoning instead.

High Altitude (3500–6500 ft): Use 9-inch pan. Before baking, place baking pan filled with 2 inches water on bottom oven rack. Place cheesecake on middle oven rack.

1 Serving: Calories 250 (Calories from Fat 170); Total Fat 19g (Saturated Fat 10g; Trans Fat 1.5g); Cholesterol 90mg; Sodium 460mg; Total Carbohydrate 14g (Dietary Fiber 0g; Sugars 4g); Protein 7g % Daily Value: Vitamin A 15%; Vitamin C 2%; Calcium 6%; Iron 6% Exchanges: 1 Starch, ¹/₂ High-Fat Meat, 3 Fat Carbohydrate Choices: 1

light up hanukkah

Hanukkah Rugelach • Hanukkah Cutouts • Cranberry Oatmeal Cookies • Chocolate Spritz • Chocolate Ganache Meringues • Chewy Chocolate–Peanut Butter Bars • Candy Bar Pie • Raspberries and Cream Snowflake Pie • Bittersweet Chocolate Tart with Kiwifruit • Coffee-Pecan Tarts • Raspberry Fudge Torte • Cherry-Almond Torte • Mocha-Hazelnut Cream-Filled Cake • Glazed Almond Amaretto Cheesecake • Praline Cream Puffs • Orange-Chocolate Bubble Bread • Savory Crescent Palmiers • Seed-Crusted Challah • Mini Reuben Turnovers • Parmesan Rounds with Lox • Olive-Feta Pinwheels • Bruschetta Appetizer Tart

hanukkah rugelach

Prep Time: **1 hour 25 minutes**   Start to Finish: **2 hours 55 minutes**   64 cookies

COOKIES

2 tablespoons granulated sugar

1 cup butter or margarine, softened

1 package (8 oz) cream cheese, softened

2 cups all-purpose flour

FILLING

$1/2$ cup finely chopped dates

$1/2$ cup finely chopped pistachio nuts

$1/3$ cup granulated sugar

2 teaspoons ground cinnamon

$1/4$ cup butter, softened

TOPPING

1 tablespoon powdered sugar

1 In large bowl, beat all cookie ingredients except flour with electric mixer on medium speed, scraping bowl occasionally, until light and fluffy. On low speed, beat in flour, scraping bowl occasionally, until well mixed. Shape dough into ball; divide into 4 pieces. Shape each piece into a ball; flatten into $1/2$-inch-thick disk. Wrap each disk in plastic wrap; refrigerate 1 hour for easier handling.

2 Heat oven to 375°F. Grease 2 cookie sheets with cooking spray. In small bowl, mix all filling ingredients until well blended.

3 Work with 1 disk of dough at a time; keep remaining dough refrigerated. On floured work surface, roll out dough with floured rolling pin to $1/8$-inch thickness, forming 12-inch round. Sprinkle $1/4$ of date-nut mixture onto round; press into dough slightly. Cut round into 16 wedges. Starting with curved edge, roll up each wedge; place point side down on cookie sheets.

4 Bake 13 to 18 minutes or until light golden brown. Immediately remove from cookie sheets; place on cooling racks. Cool completely, about 30 minutes. Sprinkle with powdered sugar.

Rugelach or rugalach are bite-size crescent-shaped cookies made with a rich cream cheese dough and filled with a variety of fillings.

High Altitude (3500–6500 ft): Bake 14 to 17 minutes.

1 Cookie: Calories 80 (Calories from Fat 50); Total Fat 5g (Saturated Fat 3g; Trans Fat 0g); Cholesterol 15mg; Sodium 35mg; Total Carbohydrate 6g (Dietary Fiber 0g; Sugars 3g); Protein 0g % Daily Value: Vitamin A 4%; Vitamin C 0%; Calcium 0%; Iron 0% Exchanges: $1/2$ Other Carbohydrate, 1 Fat Carbohydrate Choices: $1/2$

hanukkah cutouts

Prep Time: **1 hour 15 minutes**   Start to Finish: **2 hours 15 minutes**   5 dozen cookies

COOKIES

1 $1/4$ cups powdered sugar

1 cup butter or margarine,
　softened

1 teaspoon vanilla

1 egg

2 $1/2$ cups all-purpose flour

1 teaspoon baking soda

1 teaspoon cream of tartar

GLAZE

2 cups powdered sugar

2 tablespoons milk

$1/2$ teaspoon vanilla

DECORATOR FROSTING

1 cup powdered sugar

1 $1/2$ teaspoons butter or
　margarine, softened

Blue food color

1 to 2 tablespoons milk

1 In large bowl, beat 1 $1/4$ cups powdered sugar and 1 cup butter until light and fluffy. Add 1 teaspoon vanilla and the egg; blend well. Stir in flour, baking soda and cream of tartar; mix well. Cover with plastic wrap; refrigerate 1 hour for easier handling.

2 Heat oven to 375°F. On lightly floured work surface, roll out dough $1/3$ at a time to $1/8$-inch thickness. Keep remaining dough refrigerated. Cut with lightly floured 2- to 2 $1/2$-inch cookie cutters. Place 1 inch apart on ungreased cookie sheets.

3 Bake 6 to 9 minutes or until edges are light golden brown. Immediately remove from cookie sheets. Cool completely.

4 In small bowl, blend glaze ingredients until smooth, adding 2 tablespoons milk for thin spreading consistency. Spread glaze on cooled cookies. Allow glaze to set before decorating.

5 In another small bowl, mix all decorator frosting ingredients, adding enough milk for desired piping consistency. Place in decorating bag fitted with writing tip or in small resealable freezer plastic bag with one corner snipped off to make a very small hole for piping. Decorate cookies as desired.

Dreidels (a spinning top), a menorah (a nine-branched candelabrum), Star of David and round shapes to resemble gelt (coins) are favorite cutout shapes for Hanukkah celebrations.

High Altitude (3500–6500 ft): Decrease powdered sugar in cookies to 1 cup.

1 Cookie: Calories 80 (Calories from Fat 30); Total Fat 3.5g (Saturated Fat 2g; Trans Fat 0g); Cholesterol 10mg; Sodium 45mg; Total Carbohydrate 12g (Dietary Fiber 0g; Sugars 7g); Protein 0g % Daily Value: Vitamin A 2%; Vitamin C 0%; Calcium 0%; Iron 0% Exchanges: 1 Other Carbohydrate, $1/2$ Fat Carbohydrate Choices: 1

hanukkah cookie cutouts

Hanukkah, also called the "festival of lights," celebrates a miracle occurring over 2,000 years ago. With the invaders who took over the holy temple defeated, the temple was rededicated to celebrate victory. There was oil enough for only one day, but miraculously the light shone eight days! Today, menorah candles symbolize those eight nights of light.

If you can't find Hanukkah cookie cutters, make templates out of cardboard and cut around shape with sharp knife.

Cut nine candle shapes to make a cookie menorah and arrange on large flat serving platter; put a small yellow or orange candy or candy corn at the top of each for "flame."

Design your cookies! For a marbled look, paint, drizzle or pipe a contrasting frosting color on a freshly glazed or frosted cookie. Use a small brush or toothpick to swirl colors for a marbleized look. Or, "flock" cookies by sprinkling freshly glazed or frosted cookies with edible glitter or sugar.

Add more festivity to the cookie tray by adding foil-wrapped chocolate gelt and colorful confetti or pieces of curled curling ribbon.

cranberry oatmeal cookies

Prep Time: **1 hour 10 minutes**   Start to Finish: **1 hour 10 minutes**   About 7 $^1/_2$ dozen cookies

1 cup butter or margarine,
   softened

$^3/_4$ cup granulated sugar

$^3/_4$ cup packed brown sugar

$^1/_2$ cup buttermilk*

2 eggs

2 cups all-purpose flour

1 teaspoon baking powder

1 teaspoon baking soda

1 teaspoon ground cinnamon

$^1/_2$ teaspoon salt

$^1/_2$ teaspoon ground nutmeg

2 teaspoons grated orange peel

3 cups quick-cooking oats

1 $^1/_2$ cups chopped fresh or
   frozen cranberries, thawed**

1 cup chopped walnuts

1 Heat oven to 375°F. Grease cookie sheets with shortening. In large bowl, beat butter, granulated sugar and brown sugar until light and fluffy. Add buttermilk and eggs; beat well. Add flour, baking powder, baking soda, cinnamon, salt, nutmeg and orange peel; blend well. Add oats; mix well. Fold in cranberries and walnuts. Drop by teaspoonfuls onto cookie sheets.

2 Bake 8 to 10 minutes or until golden brown around edges. Cool 1 minute before removing from cookie sheets. Cool completely.

*To substitute for buttermilk, use 1 $^1/_2$ teaspoons vinegar or lemon juice plus milk to make $^1/_2$ cup.

**To chop cranberries in food processor, place in processor bowl with metal blade. Cover; process with 10 on-and-off pulses or until all berries are coarsely chopped.

Try creamy white chocolate chunks or white vanilla baking chips in place of the walnuts.

High Altitude (3500–6500 ft):
No change.

1 Cookie: Calories 70 (Calories from Fat 30); Total Fat 3g (Saturated Fat 1.5g; Trans Fat 0g); Cholesterol 10mg; Sodium 50mg; Total Carbohydrate 8g (Dietary Fiber 0g; Sugars 4g); Protein 1g % Daily Value: Vitamin A 0%; Vitamin C 0%; Calcium 0%; Iron 0% Exchanges: $^1/_2$ Other Carbohydrate, $^1/_2$ Fat Carbohydrate Choices: $^1/_2$

chocolate spritz

Prep Time: **1 hour**   Start to Finish: **1 hour 30 minutes**   5 dozen bars

1 cup granulated sugar

$^1/_2$ cup butter or margarine, softened

1 egg

2 cups all-purpose flour

2 tablespoons milk

2 oz unsweetened baking chocolate, melted, cooled

2 tablespoons powdered sugar

1 Heat oven to 375°F. In large bowl, beat granulated sugar and butter until light and fluffy. Add egg; beat well. Alternately add flour and milk to butter mixture, mixing until well combined. Add cooled chocolate; blend well. If necessary, cover with plastic wrap; refrigerate 30 minutes for easier handling.

2 Fit cookie press with serrated bar template. Place dough in cookie press; press long strips onto ungreased cookie sheets. Cut strips into 4-inch pieces.

3 Bake 5 to 7 minutes or until edges are light brown. Immediately remove from cookie sheets; cool slightly. Sprinkle with powdered sugar.

Drizzle cookies with melted white chocolate or almond bark, and sprinkle with colored sugar before the chocolate sets for a pretty sparkling look.

High Altitude (3500–6500 ft): No change.

1 Bar: Calories 50 (Calories from Fat 20); Total Fat 2g (Saturated Fat 1.5g; Trans Fat 0g); Cholesterol 10mg; Sodium 10mg; Total Carbohydrate 7g (Dietary Fiber 0g; Sugars 4g); Protein 0g % Daily Value: Vitamin A 0%; Vitamin C 0%; Calcium 0%; Iron 2% Exchanges: $^1/_2$ Other Carbohydrate, $^1/_2$ Fat Carbohydrate Choices: $^1/_2$

chocolate ganache meringues

Prep Time: **35 minutes**   Start to Finish: **1 hour 50 minutes**   12 sandwich cookies

GANACHE

$^1/_4$ cup whipping cream

3 oz bittersweet baking
chocolate, cut into pieces

2 tablespoons butter or
margarine, cut into
small pieces

MERINGUES

2 egg whites

$^1/_3$ cup granulated sugar

$^1/_3$ cup powdered sugar

$^1/_4$ cup powdered sugar

2 tablespoons unsweetened
baking cocoa

1 In small heavy saucepan, heat whipping cream over medium heat just until cream comes to a simmer. Remove from heat; stir in chocolate until melted. Stir in butter pieces, a few at a time, until melted. Refrigerate until thickened.

2 Heat oven to 200°F. Line cookie sheet with parchment paper. In medium bowl, beat egg whites with electric mixer on medium speed until soft peaks form. Gradually add granulated sugar, beating at high speed just until stiff peaks form. Fold in $^1/_3$ cup powdered sugar.

3 In small bowl, mix $^1/_4$ cup powdered sugar and the cocoa. Fold cocoa mixture, $^1/_3$ at a time, into beaten egg whites. Spoon mixture into decorating bag fitted with star tip. Pipe into twenty-four 1 $^1/_2$-inch rounds on cookie sheet.

4 Bake 1 to 1 $^1/_4$ hours or until crisp. Cool completely, about 5 minutes.

5 For each sandwich cookie, spread chilled ganache on flat side of 1 meringue; top with second meringue.

Meringues that are the same size look better when sandwiched together—just like they came straight from a pastry shop! It's so easy to do. Just trace 1 $^1/_2$-inch circles on parchment paper; turn the paper over and pipe the meringue on the other side.

High Altitude (3500–6500 ft): Decrease granulated sugar to $^1/_4$ cup. In step 2, heat oven to 225°F. In step 4, bake 1 $^1/_4$ to 1 $^1/_2$ hours.

1 Sandwich Cookie: Calories 130 (Calories from Fat 70); Total Fat 7g (Saturated Fat 4.5g; Trans Fat 0g); Cholesterol 10mg; Sodium 25mg; Total Carbohydrate 14g (Dietary Fiber 1g; Sugars 11g); Protein 2g % Daily Value: Vitamin A 2%; Vitamin C 0%; Calcium 0%; Iron 8% Exchanges: 1 Other Carbohydrate, 1 $^1/_2$ Fat Carbohydrate Choices: 1

chewy chocolate–peanut butter bars

extra easy

| Prep Time: **15 minutes** | Start to Finish: **2 hours 45 minutes** | 36 bars |

1 roll (16.5 oz) refrigerated sugar cookies

1 can (14 oz) sweetened condensed milk (not evaporated)

1 cup crunchy peanut butter

1 teaspoon vanilla

3 egg yolks

1 bag (12 oz) semisweet chocolate chips (2 cups)

1 Heat oven to 350°F. Spray 13 × 9-inch pan with cooking spray. Cut cookie dough in half crosswise. Cut each section in half lengthwise. With floured fingers, press dough in bottom of pan to form crust. Bake 10 minutes.

2 Meanwhile, in medium bowl, mix condensed milk, peanut butter, vanilla and egg yolks until smooth.

3 Spoon milk mixture evenly over partially baked crust; carefully spread. Bake 20 to 25 minutes longer or until set.

4 Sprinkle with chocolate chips; let stand 3 minutes to soften. Spread chocolate evenly over top. Cool completely, about 1 $^1/_2$ hours. Refrigerate 30 minutes to set chocolate. For bars, cut into 6 rows by 6 rows.

Bake a couple pans of these yummy, chewy, ooey-gooey bars for all the kids' Hanukkah festivities—they will think you're the best!

High Altitude (3500–6500 ft): In large bowl, break up cookie dough. Stir or knead in 2 tablespoons all-purpose flour before pressing dough in bottom of pan to form crust. Bake crust 15 minutes.

1 Bar: Calories 190 (Calories from Fat 90); Total Fat 10g (Saturated Fat 3.5g; Trans Fat 0.5g); Cholesterol 25mg; Sodium 85mg; Total Carbohydrate 21g (Dietary Fiber 1g; Sugars 16g); Protein 4g % Daily Value: Vitamin A 0%; Vitamin C 0%; Calcium 4%; Iron 4% Exchanges: $^1/_2$ Starch, 1 Other Carbohydrate, 2 Fat Carbohydrate Choices: 1 $^1/_2$

candy bar pie

Prep Time: **20 minutes**　　Start to Finish: **3 hours 40 minutes**　　10 servings

CRUST

1 refrigerated pie crust (from 15-
　oz box), softened as directed
　on box

FILLING

5 bars (2.07 oz each) chocolate-
　covered peanut, caramel and
　nougat candy

$^1/_2$ cup sugar

4 packages (3 oz each) cream
　cheese, softened

2 eggs

$^1/_3$ cup sour cream

$^1/_3$ cup creamy peanut butter

TOPPING

3 tablespoons whipping cream

$^2/_3$ cup milk chocolate chips

1 Heat oven to 450°F. Place pie crust in 9-inch glass pie plate as directed on box for One-Crust Filled Pie. Bake 5 to 7 minutes or until very light golden brown. Remove from oven; cool. Reduce oven temperature to 325°F.

2 Cut candy bars in half lengthwise; cut into $^1/_4$-inch pieces. Place candy bar pieces over bottom of partially baked crust. In small bowl, beat sugar and cream cheese until smooth. Beat in 1 egg at a time until well blended. Add sour cream and peanut butter, beating until mixture is smooth. Pour over candy bar pieces. Bake 30 to 40 minutes or until center is set. Cool completely.

3 In small saucepan, heat whipping cream until very warm. Remove from heat; stir in chocolate chips until chips are melted and mixture is smooth. Spread over top of pie. Refrigerate 2 to 3 hours before serving. Store in refrigerator.

Chopped candy bars are topped with a rich, lightly flavored peanut butter layer and milk chocolate. Garnish each serving of pie with a dollop of whipped cream, and gently arrange a few additional pieces of chopped candy on the whipped cream.

High Altitude (3500–6500 ft): In step 1, bake 6 to 8 minutes. In step 2, bake 35 to 45 minutes or until set.

1 Serving: Calories 560 (Calories from Fat 330); Total Fat 37g (Saturated Fat 18g; Trans Fat 0.5g); Cholesterol 95mg; Sodium 320mg; Total Carbohydrate 48g (Dietary Fiber 2g; Sugars 34g); Protein 9g % Daily Value: Vitamin A 15%; Vitamin C 0%; Calcium 8%; Iron 6% Exchanges: 1 Starch, 2 Other Carbohydrate, 1 High-Fat Meat, 5 $^1/_2$ Fat Carbohydrate Choices: 3

raspberries and cream snowflake pie

Prep Time: **45 minutes**   Start to Finish: **3 hours 45 minutes**   8 servings

CRUST

1 box (15 oz) refrigerated pie
crusts, softened as directed
on box

FILLING

1 can (21 oz) raspberry pie filling

1 package (8 oz) cream cheese,
softened

1 can (14 oz) sweetened
condensed milk (not
evaporated)

$1/3$ cup lemon juice

$1/2$ teaspoon almond extract

$1/2$ to 1 teaspoon powdered
sugar

1 Heat oven to 450°F. Make pie crust as directed on box for One-Crust Baked Shell using 9-inch glass pie plate. Bake 9 to 11 minutes or until lightly browned. Cool.

2 To make snowflake crust, unroll remaining crust onto ungreased cookie sheet. Cut crust into 7 $1/2$-inch diameter round; discard scraps. Fold round in half, then in half again on cookie sheet. With knife, cut designs from folded and curved edges; discard scraps. Unfold. Bake 6 to 8 minutes or until lightly browned. Cool completely.

3 Reserve $1/2$ cup raspberry filling; spoon remaining filling into cooled baked shell. In large bowl, beat cream cheese until light and fluffy. Add condensed milk; blend well. Add lemon juice and almond extract; stir until thickened. Spoon over raspberry filling in crust. Refrigerate 1 hour.

4 Spoon reserved $1/2$ cup raspberry filling around edge of pie. Place snowflake crust over top. Refrigerate several hours.

5 Just before serving, sprinkle with powdered sugar. Store in refrigerator.

Remember when you were a kid and cut paper dolls or snowflake designs out of paper? This beautiful pie uses that same idea, except you do the cutting on pie crust instead. No need to be intricate—a simple design will look great.

High Altitude (3500–6500 ft):
No change.

1 Serving: Calories 650 (Calories from Fat 220); Total Fat 25g (Saturated Fat 13g; Trans Fat 0g); Cholesterol 55mg; Sodium 340mg; Total Carbohydrate 99g (Dietary Fiber 0g; Sugars 64g); Protein 6g % Daily Value: Vitamin A 10%; Vitamin C 8%; Calcium 20%; Iron 4% Exchanges: 2 Starch, 4 $1/2$ Other Carbohydrate, 5 Fat Carbohydrate Choices: 6 $1/2$

bittersweet chocolate tart with kiwifruit

| Prep Time: **35 minutes** | Start to Finish: **2 hours** | 12 servings |

CRUST

1 refrigerated pie crust (from 15-oz box), softened as directed on box

FILLING

6 oz bittersweet baking chocolate, chopped

6 tablespoons butter or margarine

2 tablespoons milk

2 tablespoons corn syrup

$^1/_2$ teaspoon vanilla

4 eggs

GARNISH

2 kiwifruit, peeled, sliced

$^1/_2$ cup whipping cream, whipped

1 Heat oven to 450°F. Make pie crust as directed on box for One-Crust Baked Shell using 10-inch tart pan with removable bottom or 9-inch glass pie plate. Bake 9 to 11 minutes or until lightly browned. Cool. Reduce oven temperature to 325°F.

2 In medium saucepan, melt chocolate and butter over low heat, stirring until smooth. Set aside to cool slightly.

3 In medium bowl, beat all remaining filling ingredients. Gradually add egg mixture to chocolate mixture, stirring until well combined. Pour into partially baked shell.

4 Bake 15 to 20 minutes or until set. Cool completely, about 45 minutes. Garnish each serving with kiwifruit and whipped cream. Store in refrigerator.

Sophisticated, elegant and so easy to make. Bittersweet chocolate is no longer a specialty gourmet ingredient; it's made by national chocolate manufacturers and available in most large grocery stores. In addition to the kiwifruit and whipped cream garnish, a single fresh raspberry on each serving would look smashing!

High Altitude (3500–6500 ft): No change.

1 Serving: Calories 300 (Calories from Fat 210); Total Fat 23g (Saturated Fat 12g; Trans Fat 0g); Cholesterol 100mg; Sodium 150mg; Total Carbohydrate 18g (Dietary Fiber 3g; Sugars 3g); Protein 4g % Daily Value: Vitamin A 8%; Vitamin C 10%; Calcium 4%; Iron 15% Exchanges: 1 Starch, 4 $^1/_2$ Fat Carbohydrate Choices: 1

coffee-pecan tarts

Prep Time: **25 minutes**   Start to Finish: **1 hour 15 minutes**   4 tarts

1 refrigerated pie crust (from 15-
oz box), softened as directed
on box

4 foil tart pans (5 inch)

Sugar or coarse white sparkling
sugar

1 egg

1/4 cup sugar

1/4 cup light corn syrup

2 tablespoons coffee-flavored
liqueur or cold strong coffee

Dash salt

$^1/_2$ teaspoon vanilla

$^1/_2$ cup pecan halves

$^1/_2$ cup whipped cream or
whipped topping, if desired

1 Heat oven to 375°F. Place pie crust flat on lightly floured surface. With 4 $^1/_2$-inch round cookie cutter or top of 4 $^1/_2$-inch diameter bowl as pattern, cut 4 rounds from pie crust. Fit rounds in bottom and part way up sides of foil tart pans. With fork, prick bottoms and sides generously. Place pans on ungreased cookie sheet.

2 If desired, cut small star shapes from remaining pie crust; place on same cookie sheet with tart pans. Prick stars with fork; sprinkle lightly with sugar.

3 Bake tart shells and stars 6 to 8 minutes or just until shells are dry and stars are golden brown.

4 Meanwhile, in medium bowl, beat egg with wire whisk. Beat in $^1/_4$ cup sugar, the corn syrup, liqueur, salt and vanilla.

5 Remove partially baked tart shells and baked stars from oven. Remove stars from cookie sheet. Arrange pecans evenly in shells. Pour egg mixture evenly over pecans.

6 Bake 16 to 20 minutes longer or until crusts are golden brown and center is set. Cool 30 minutes. Remove tarts from pans. Top each with whipped cream; garnish with baked pie crust stars.

High Altitude (3500–6500 ft): Bake tart shells and stars 8 to 10 minutes. Add 1 tablespoon all-purpose flour to egg mixture. Bake tarts 16 to 18 minutes.

1 Tart: Calories 480 (Calories from Fat 220); Total Fat 24g (Saturated Fat 6g; Trans Fat 0g); Cholesterol 60mg; Sodium 300mg; Total Carbohydrate 61g (Dietary Fiber 1g; Sugars 25g); Protein 3g % Daily Value: Vitamin A 0%; Vitamin C 0%; Calcium 0%; Iron 2% Exchanges: 1 Starch, 3 Other Carbohydrate, 4 $^1/_2$ Fat Carbohydrate Choices: 4

raspberry fudge torte

Prep Time: **45 minutes**   Start to Finish: **3 hours 30 minutes**   12 servings

CAKE

1 box (1 lb 2.25 oz) devil's food
   cake mix with pudding

1 container (8 oz) sour cream

$^3/_4$ cup water

$^1/_3$ cup vegetable oil

1 teaspoon vanilla

3 eggs

1 cup miniature semisweet
   chocolate chips

RASPBERRY CREAM

1 box (10 oz) frozen raspberries
   in syrup, thawed

2 tablespoons sugar

4 teaspoons cornstarch

$^1/_2$ cup whipping cream, whipped

FROSTING

$^3/_4$ cup chocolate creamy ready-
   to-spread frosting (from 1-lb
   container)

$^1/_2$ pint (1 cup) fresh raspberries

Fresh mint sprigs, if desired

1. Heat oven to 350°F (if using dark or nonstick pans, heat oven to 325°F). Grease and flour two 9-inch round cake pans with shortening. In large bowl, beat all cake ingredients except chocolate chips with electric mixer on low speed 30 seconds. Beat on medium speed 2 minutes, scraping bowl occasionally. Stir in chocolate chips. Pour batter into pans.

2. Bake 30 to 40 minutes or until toothpick inserted in center comes out clean. Cool 15 minutes. Remove cakes from pans; place on cooling racks. Cool completely, about 1 hour. (Wrap and freeze 1 cake layer for later use.)

3. Place strainer over small saucepan; add raspberries. Press through strainer with back of spoon to remove seeds; discard seeds. Stir sugar and cornstarch into raspberries until smooth. Cook over low heat, stirring constantly, until mixture is bubbly and thickened. Boil 1 minute. Place plastic wrap over surface of mixture; refrigerate until cold, about 30 minutes. Fold in whipped cream.

4. To assemble torte, place cake layer, top side down, on serving plate. Spread with thin layer of frosting. Top with raspberry cream, spreading to within $^1/_2$ inch of edge. Frost side of torte with remaining frosting. Refrigerate at least 1 hour before serving.

5. Just before serving, arrange fresh raspberries around top edge of torte. Garnish with additional fresh raspberries and the mint sprigs. Store in refrigerator.

High Altitude (3500–6500 ft):
No change.

1 Serving: Calories 500 (Calories from Fat 220); Total Fat 25g (Saturated Fat 10g; Trans Fat 2g); Cholesterol 75mg; Sodium 420mg; Total Carbohydrate 64g (Dietary Fiber 4g; Sugars 45g); Protein 5g % Daily Value: Vitamin A 6%; Vitamin C 6%; Calcium 8%; Iron 15% Exchanges: 1 $^1/_2$ Starch, 2 $^1/_2$ Other Carbohydrate, 5 Fat Carbohydrate Choices: 4

cherry-almond torte

Prep Time: **25 minutes** Start to Finish: **3 hours 35 minutes** 12 servings

CHERRY MIXTURE

1 can (21 oz) cherry pie filling

1 tablespoon cornstarch

CAKE

1 box (1 lb 2.25 oz) yellow cake
  mix with pudding

1 1/4 cups water

1/3 cup vegetable oil

2 teaspoons almond extract

3 eggs

**WHIPPED CREAM AND
  ALMOND CREAM**

1 1/2 cups whipping cream

1 container (8 oz) cream cheese
  spread, softened

1/2 cup sliced almonds, toasted*

*To toast almonds, bake uncovered
in ungreased shallow pan in 350°F
oven 5 to 7 minutes, stirring
occasionally, until light brown.

1 Heat oven to 350°F (if using dark or nonstick pans, heat oven to 325°F). In 2-quart saucepan, mix pie filling and cornstarch. Heat over medium heat about 7 minutes, stirring constantly, until mixture is boiling. Set aside.

2 Grease bottoms only of two 9-inch round pans with shortening. In large bowl, beat cake ingredients with electric mixer on low speed 30 seconds. Beat on medium speed 2 minutes, scraping bowl occasionally. Pour and spread batter evenly into pans.

3 Bake 24 to 29 minutes or until toothpick inserted in center comes out clean. Cool 10 minutes; remove from pans and place on cooling racks. Cool completely, about 30 minutes.

4 In medium bowl, beat whipping cream with electric mixer on high speed until soft peaks form. Beat in cream cheese until fluffy. Reserve 1/2 cup whipped cream mixture for garnish. Stir almonds into remaining cream mixture.

5 With serrated knife, cut each cake layer in half horizontally. To assemble torte, place 1 half cake layer on serving plate; spread with 1 cup almond cream. Top with second half layer; spread with 1 cup cherry mixture. Top with third half layer; spread with 1 cup almond cream. Place remaining half layer on top.

6 Spoon remaining cherry mixture on top of torte, spreading almost to edge. Frost side of torte with remaining 1 1/4 cups almond cream. Spoon reserved 1/2 cup whipped cream mixture into decorating bag with large star tip. Pipe cream around top edge of torte. Refrigerate about 2 hours. Store in refrigerator.

High Altitude (3500–6500 ft):
No change.

1 Serving: Calories 480 (Calories from Fat 260); Total Fat 29g (Saturated Fat 13g; Trans Fat 1.5g); Cholesterol 105mg; Sodium 360mg; Total Carbohydrate 50g (Dietary Fiber 1g; Sugars 32g); Protein 6g % Daily Value: Vitamin A 15%; Vitamin C 2%; Calcium 10%; Iron 8% Exchanges: 1 1/2 Starch, 2 Other Carbohydrate, 5 1/2 Fat Carbohydrate Choices: 3

mocha-hazelnut cream-filled cake

Prep Time: **35 minutes** | Start to Finish: **3 hours** | 16 servings

1 box (1 lb 2.25 oz) butter recipe chocolate cake mix with pudding

1 1/3 cups water

1/2 cup butter, softened

3 eggs

2 teaspoons instant coffee granules or crystals

2 bags (12 oz each) semisweet chocolate chips (4 cups)

1 bottle (16 oz) refrigerated hazelnut-flavor coffee creamer

1 package (8 oz) cream cheese, softened

2 tablespoons chopped hazelnuts (filberts)

1 Heat oven to 350°F (if using dark or nonstick pans, heat oven to 325°F). Grease bottoms only of two 9-inch round pans with shortening. In large bowl, beat cake mix, water, butter, eggs and coffee granules with electric mixer on low speed 30 seconds or until blended. Beat on medium speed 2 minutes, scraping bowl occasionally. Pour batter into pan.

2 Bake 28 to 33 minutes or until toothpick inserted in center comes out clean. Cool 10 minutes; invert onto cooling racks.

3 In 3-quart saucepan, cook chocolate chips and coffee creamer over medium-low heat about 8 minutes, stirring constantly, until melted. Remove from heat; beat in cream cheese with wire whisk until smooth. Cover; refrigerate about 30 minutes.

4 In small microwavable bowl, reserve 1/2 cup of the chocolate mixture. Beat remaining mixture with electric mixer on medium-high speed 8 minutes or until light and fluffy.

5 Place 1 cake layer on serving plate, rounded side down. Spread 1-inch-thick layer of frosting over cake. Top with second cake layer, rounded side up. Spread frosting on side and top of cake.

6 Microwave reserved 1/2 cup chocolate mixture on High 30 seconds or until soft; spread over top of cake. Sprinkle hazelnuts around top edge. Cover loosely; refrigerate at least 1 hour before serving. Store in refrigerator.

High Altitude (3500–6500 ft): No change.

1 Serving: Calories 550 (Calories from Fat 280); Total Fat 31g (Saturated Fat 16g; Trans Fat 1g); Cholesterol 70mg; Sodium 370mg; Total Carbohydrate 63g (Dietary Fiber 4g; Sugars 43g); Protein 6g % Daily Value: Vitamin A 8%; Vitamin C 0%; Calcium 6%; Iron 15% Exchanges: 1 Starch, 3 Other Carbohydrate, 6 Fat Carbohydrate Choices: 4

glazed almond amaretto cheesecake

| Prep Time: **20 minutes** | Start to Finish: **8 hours** | 16 servings |

TOPPING

$^1/_2$ cup sugar

$^1/_4$ cup water

1 cup sliced almonds

1 teaspoon amaretto

CRUST

2 cups graham cracker crumbs
(about 32 squares)

$^1/_4$ cup finely chopped almonds

$^1/_3$ cup butter or margarine,
melted

FILLING

2 packages (8 oz each) cream
cheese, softened

1 cup sugar

3 eggs

1 cup sour cream

$^1/_2$ cup whipping cream

$^1/_4$ cup amaretto

$^1/_2$ teaspoon almond extract

1 In small saucepan, heat $^1/_2$ cup sugar and the water to boiling; boil 2 minutes. Remove from heat. Stir in sliced almonds and 1 teaspoon amaretto. With slotted spoon, remove almonds and place on waxed paper; separate with fork. Cool.

2 Heat oven to 350°F. In medium bowl, mix all crust ingredients. Press mixture in bottom and 1 $^1/_2$ inches up side of ungreased 10-inch springform pan.

3 In large bowl, beat cream cheese and 1 cup sugar with electric mixer on medium speed until smooth and creamy. At low speed, beat in 1 egg at a time until well blended. Add all remaining filling ingredients; blend well. Pour into crust-lined pan.

4 Bake 45 to 60 minutes; arrange sliced almonds in 2-inch-wide circle around outer edge of cheesecake. Bake 15 minutes longer or until center is set. Cool 15 minutes. Run knife around edge of pan; carefully remove side of pan. Cool completely. Refrigerate several hours or overnight before serving. Store in refrigerator.

Relax and enjoy—make this cheesecake the day before your party. The crunchy topping of amaretto-glazed almonds is unique and snazzy.

High Altitude (3500–6500 ft):
No change.

1 Serving: Calories 370 (Calories from Fat 220); Total Fat 25g (Saturated Fat 13g; Trans Fat 1g); Cholesterol 100mg; Sodium 190mg; Total Carbohydrate 30g (Dietary Fiber 1g; Sugars 25g); Protein 6g % Daily Value: Vitamin A 15%; Vitamin C 0%; Calcium 6%; Iron 6% Exchanges: 1 Starch, 1 Other Carbohydrate, $^1/_2$ High-Fat Meat, 4 Fat Carbohydrate Choices: 2

praline cream puffs

Prep Time: **30 minutes**   Start to Finish: **1 hour 30 minutes**   12 cream puffs

CREAM PUFFS

1 cup water

$1/2$ cup butter or margarine

1 cup all-purpose flour

$1/2$ teaspoon salt

4 eggs

TOASTED PECAN SAUCE

$1/2$ cup butter or margarine

$1 1/4$ cups packed brown sugar

$1/4$ cup corn syrup

$1/2$ cup whipping cream

1 cup chopped pecans, toasted*

FILLING

1 quart (4 cups) vanilla or butter
    pecan ice cream

Cream puffs may seem like a hard-to-make mystery. Reality check—super easy! No special ingredients or equipment required—just flour, water, butter, salt and eggs along with a spoon and saucepan.

1. Heat oven to 400°F. Grease cookie sheets with shortening. In medium saucepan, heat water and $1/2$ cup butter to boiling over medium heat. Stir in flour and salt; cook, stirring constantly, until mixture leaves side of pan in smooth ball.

2. Remove from heat. Beat in 1 egg at a time until mixture is smooth and glossy. DO NOT OVERBEAT.

3. Spoon 12 mounds of dough (about $1/4$ cup each) 3 inches apart onto cookie sheet.

4. Bake 30 to 35 minutes or until golden brown. Prick puffs with sharp knife to allow steam to escape. Remove from cookie sheets; cool completely.

5. To make sauce, in medium saucepan, melt $1/2$ cup butter. Stir in brown sugar and corn syrup. Heat to boiling; boil 1 minute, stirring constantly. Gradually stir in whipping cream; return to boiling. Remove from heat. Stir in pecans. Keep warm.

6. To serve, place each puff on serving plate; slice in half horizontally. Spoon about $1/3$ cup ice cream into bottom half of puff. Replace top half of puff; drizzle with sauce.

*To toast pecans, bake uncovered in ungreased shallow pan in 350°F oven 6 to 10 minutes, stirring occasionally, until light brown.

High Altitude (3500–6500 ft):
No change.

1 Cream Puff: Calories 510 (Calories from Fat 290); Total Fat 32g (Saturated Fat 16g; Trans Fat 1g); Cholesterol 145mg; Sodium 290mg; Total Carbohydrate 49g (Dietary Fiber 2g; Sugars 34g); Protein 6g % Daily Value: Vitamin A 20%; Vitamin C 0%; Calcium 10%; Iron 8% Exchanges: 1 Starch, 2 Other Carbohydrate, $1/2$ High-Fat Meat, 5 $1/2$ Fat Carbohydrate Choices: 3

orange-chocolate bubble bread

| Prep Time: **10 minutes** | Start to Finish: **1 hour** | 12 servings |

4 tablespoons butter or margarine, softened

2 cans (13.9 oz each) refrigerated orange flavor sweet rolls with icing

$1/2$ cup orange marmalade

$1/4$ cup miniature semisweet chocolate chips

1 Heat oven to 375°F. Generously grease 12-cup fluted tube (bundt cake) pan with 1 tablespoon of the butter. In small microwavable bowl, microwave remaining butter on High 30 seconds or until melted; stir.

2 Separate dough into 16 rolls. Cut each in half crosswise. Place half of the roll pieces, cut edge down, in pan. Spoon and spread half of marmalade over rolls, avoiding touching sides of pan. Drizzle with half of melted butter. Layer with remaining roll pieces and marmalade. Sprinkle with chocolate chips. Drizzle with remaining butter.

3 Bake 22 to 32 minutes or until rolls are golden brown and dough appears done when slightly pulled apart. Cool in pan 2 minutes. Invert onto serving platter. Cool 15 minutes.

4 Stir icing to soften. Spread over warm bread. Slice or pull apart bread to serve.

Generously grease the pan's grooves. If the marmalade sticks to the pan after baking, remove it with a small spatula and spread it on the baked bread. This warm sticky bread is best served right away.

High Altitude (3500–6500 ft): Bake 28 to 33 minutes.

1 Serving: Calories 320 (Calories from Fat 130); Total Fat 14g (Saturated Fat 5g; Trans Fat 3g); Cholesterol 10mg; Sodium 490mg; Total Carbohydrate 45g (Dietary Fiber 1g; Sugars 22g); Protein 3g % Daily Value: Vitamin A 2%; Vitamin C 0%; Calcium 0%; Iron 10% Exchanges: 1 Starch, 2 Other Carbohydrate, 2 $1/2$ Fat Carbohydrate Choices: 3

savory crescent palmiers

| Prep Time: **15 minutes** | Start to Finish: **30 minutes** | 16 appetizers |

2 tablespoons grated Parmesan
cheese

1 can (8 oz) refrigerated crescent
dinner rolls

2 tablespoons yellow mustard

$^1/_8$ teaspoon onion powder

1 Heat oven to 375°F. Lightly grease cookie sheets with shortening. Sprinkle cutting board or waxed paper with cheese. Separate dough into 4 rectangles; firmly press perforations to seal. Lightly press dough into cheese.

2 In small bowl, blend mustard and onion powder. Brush rectangles with mustard mixture. Using 2 rectangles, place 1 rectangle, mustard side up, on top of the other. Starting with shortest sides, roll up both ends jelly-roll fashion to meet in center; cut into 8 slices. Repeat with remaining rectangles. Place, cut side down, 2 inches apart on cookie sheets.

3 Bake 6 to 12 minutes or until deep golden brown. Gently re-coil if necessary. Immediately remove from cookie sheets. Serve warm.

Not only do these flaky pastries make a tasty little appetizer, but they're also great served with soup, stew, chili or salad.

High Altitude (3500–6500 ft):
No change.

1 Appetizer: Calories 60 (Calories from Fat 30); Total Fat 3.5g (Saturated Fat 1g; Trans Fat 1g); Cholesterol 0mg; Sodium 125mg; Total Carbohydrate 6g (Dietary Fiber 0g; Sugars 1g); Protein 2g % Daily Value: Vitamin A 0%; Vitamin C 0%; Calcium 0%; Iron 0% Exchanges: $^1/_2$ Starch, $^1/_2$ Fat Carbohydrate Choices: $^1/_2$

seed-crusted challah

Prep Time: **40 minutes**   Start to Finish: **1 hour 40 minutes**   1 loaf (14 slices)

BREAD

1 $^3/_4$ to 2 $^1/_4$ cups all-purpose
   flour

2 tablespoons packed brown
   sugar

1 teaspoon salt

1 package fast-acting dry yeast

1 cup water

2 tablespoons butter or
   margarine

1 egg

$^2/_3$ cup whole wheat flour

1 egg yolk

1 tablespoon water

SEED MIXTURE

1 teaspoon poppy seed

1 teaspoon sesame seed

$^1/_2$ teaspoon fennel seed

$^1/_2$ teaspoon caraway seed

$^1/_8$ teaspoon celery, cumin
   or dill seed

1 Grease cookie sheet with shortening. In large bowl, mix 1 $^1/_2$ cups of the all-purpose flour, the brown sugar, salt and yeast.

2 In small saucepan, heat 1 cup water and the butter until very warm (120°F to 130°F). Add warm liquid and egg to flour mixture; beat with electric mixer on low speed until moistened. Beat 3 minutes on medium speed. By hand, stir in whole wheat flour and additional $^1/_4$ to $^3/_4$ cup all-purpose flour until dough pulls cleanly away from side of bowl. Cover; let rest 10 minutes.

3 On floured surface, knead dough about 25 times until smooth. Divide dough into 3 equal parts. Roll each part into 12-inch rope. Place ropes together on cookie sheet. Braid ropes gently and loosely, starting in middle; do not stretch. Punch ends; tuck ends under braid securely. Cover loosely; let rise in warm place (80°F to 85°F) until doubled in size, 30 to 40 minutes.

4 Heat oven to 375°F. In small bowl, beat egg yolk and 1 tablespoon water. In another small bowl, mix all seed mixture ingredients. Brush braid with egg yolk mixture; sprinkle with seed mixture.

5 Bake 20 to 25 minutes or until loaf sounds hollow when lightly tapped. Immediately remove from cookie sheet. Cool on cooling rack.

Challah, the traditional Jewish Sabbath braid, is made with a wonderful, easy-to-handle egg dough. Sometimes the bread is shaped in different ways—in a circle, coiled or like a bird—to signify different Jewish holidays or events.

High Altitude (3500–6500 ft):
No change.

1 Slice: Calories 110 (Calories from Fat 25); Total Fat 3g (Saturated Fat 1.5g; Trans Fat 0g); Cholesterol 35mg; Sodium 190mg; Total Carbohydrate 18g (Dietary Fiber 1g; Sugars 2g); Protein 3g % Daily Value: Vitamin A 0%; Vitamin C 0%; Calcium 0%; Iron 6% Exchanges: 1 Starch, $^1/_2$ Fat Carbohydrate Choices: 1

mini reuben turnovers

| Prep Time: **30 minutes** | Start to Finish: **45 minutes** | 24 appetizers |

2 oz corned beef (from deli), cut into pieces

$1/4$ cup shredded Swiss cheese (1 oz)

2 tablespoons well-drained sauerkraut, squeezed dry with paper towel

2 tablespoons stone-ground mustard

1 can (8 oz) refrigerated crescent dinner rolls

1 egg, beaten, if desired

Thousand Island dressing, if desired

1 Heat oven to 375°F. In food processor bowl with metal blade, place corned beef, cheese, sauerkraut and mustard. Cover; process with on-and-off pulses until finely chopped.

2 Remove half of dough in rolled section from can; refrigerate remaining half of dough in can. Unroll half of dough and separate into 2 rectangles; press each into $7 \, 1/2 \times 5$-inch rectangle, firmly pressing perforations to seal. Cut each rectangle into six $2 \, 1/2$-inch squares.

3 Place 1 teaspoon corned beef mixture on each square. Fold 1 corner to opposite corner, forming triangle and pressing edges to seal; place on ungreased cookie sheet. With fork, prick top of each to allow steam to escape. Brush tops with egg. Repeat with remaining half of dough and corned beef mixture.

4 Bake 9 to 14 minutes or until golden brown. Immediately remove from cookie sheet. Serve warm with dressing.

If corned beef isn't your favorite, try Mini Rachel Turnovers by substituting cooked turkey for the corned beef.

High Altitude (3500–6500 ft): No change.

1 Appetizer: Calories 45 (Calories from Fat 25); Total Fat 3g (Saturated Fat 1g; Trans Fat 0.5g); Cholesterol 0mg; Sodium 140mg; Total Carbohydrate 4g (Dietary Fiber 0g; Sugars 0g); Protein 1g % Daily Value: Vitamin A 0%; Vitamin C 0%; Calcium 0%; Iron 0% Exchanges: $1/2$ Starch, $1/2$ Fat Carbohydrate Choices: 0

parmesan rounds with lox

Prep Time: **10 minutes** Start to Finish: **25 minutes** 16 appetizers

1 cup shredded Parmesan or
  Asiago cheese (4 oz)

$^1/_4$ teaspoon coarse ground black
  pepper

3 oz lox (cold-smoked salmon)

2 tablespoons crème fraîche or
  sour cream

Fresh dill sprigs

1 Heat oven to 400°F. For each round, spoon 2 teaspoons cheese onto ungreased cookie sheet; pat into 2-inch round. Place rounds 2 inches apart. Sprinkle each with pepper.

2 Bake 6 to 8 minutes or until edges are light golden brown. DO NOT OVERBAKE. Immediately remove from cookie sheet; place on cooling racks. Cool completely, about 5 minutes.

3 To serve, top each round with lox, about $^1/_4$ teaspoon crème fraîche and dill sprig. Serve immediately, or cover and refrigerate until serving time.

What a great idea! Instead of the usual baguette slices, baked cheese forms into delicious little holders. Crème fraîche—a mature French cream—is convenient and versatile; it can be boiled without curdling, which makes it easy to use in cooked recipes.

High Altitude (3500–6500 ft):
No change.

1 Appetizer: Calories 35 (Calories from Fat 20); Total Fat 2.5g (Saturated Fat 1.5g; Trans Fat 0g); Cholesterol 5mg; Sodium 160mg; Total Carbohydrate 0g (Dietary Fiber 0g; Sugars 0g); Protein 4g % Daily Value: Vitamin A 0%; Vitamin C 0%; Calcium 8%; Iron 0% Exchanges: $^1/_2$ Medium-Fat Meat Carbohydrate Choices: 0

olive-feta pinwheels

Prep Time: **20 minutes**   Start to Finish: **40 minutes**   16 appetizers

1 can (8 oz) refrigerated crescent
   dinner rolls

2 tablespoons cream cheese
   spread (from 8-oz container)

$^1/_4$ cup crumbled feta cheese
   (1 oz)

$^1/_4$ cup chopped pitted kalamata
   olives

2 tablespoons chopped fresh
   oregano leaves or parsley

1 Heat oven to 350°F. Spray cookie sheet with cooking spray. Unroll dough and separate into 2 long rectangles; press each into 12 × 4-inch rectangle, firmly pressing perforations to seal.

2 Spread cream cheese over each rectangle. Sprinkle evenly with feta cheese, olives and oregano.

3 Starting with 1 short side, roll up each rectangle. With serrated knife, cut each roll into 8 slices; place cut side down on cookie sheet.

4 Bake 15 to 20 minutes or until edges are golden brown. Immediately remove from cookie sheet. Serve warm.

Try one of the flavored feta cheeses—basil-tomato or cracked pepper would be especially good in these appetizers. Arrange the pinwheels on a serving platter with grape tomatoes and whole pitted kalamata olives.

High Altitude (3500–6500 ft):
Bake 13 to 18 minutes.

1 Appetizer: Calories 70 (Calories from Fat 35); Total Fat 4g (Saturated Fat 1.5g; Trans Fat 1g); Cholesterol 0mg; Sodium 160mg; Total Carbohydrate 6g (Dietary Fiber 0g; Sugars 1g); Protein 1g % Daily Value: Vitamin A 0%; Vitamin C 0%; Calcium 0%; Iron 2% Exchanges: $^1/_2$ Starch, $^1/_2$ Fat Carbohydrate Choices: $^1/_2$

bruschetta appetizer tart

extra easy

Prep Time: **15 minutes**	Start to Finish: **25 minutes**	16 appetizers

1 refrigerated pie crust (from 15-oz box), softened as directed on box

1 cup chopped plum (Roma) tomatoes

$^1/_3$ cup chopped fresh basil leaves

2 teaspoons olive oil

1 clove garlic, finely chopped or $^1/_4$ teaspoon garlic powder

$^1/_2$ cup shredded Parmesan cheese (2 oz)

1 Heat oven to 425°F. Remove crust from pouch; unroll on ungreased cookie sheet. Bake 6 to 8 minutes or until light golden brown.

2 In medium bowl, mix remaining ingredients except cheese. Spread over partially baked crust. Sprinkle with cheese.

3 Bake 7 to 10 minutes longer or until cheese is melted and crust is golden brown. Cut into wedges.

Refrigerated pie crust creates a thin, flaky, crisp crust to hold the traditional bruschetta toppings. Add some flair to the baked tart by scattering small fresh basil leaves over the top, or garnish individual wedges with the basil leaves.

High Altitude (3500–6500 ft): No change.

1 Appetizer: Calories 80 (Calories from Fat 45); Total Fat 5g (Saturated Fat 2g; Trans Fat 0g); Cholesterol 0mg; Sodium 110mg; Total Carbohydrate 7g (Dietary Fiber 0g; Sugars 0g); Protein 1g % Daily Value: Vitamin A 4%; Vitamin C 0%; Calcium 4%; Iron 0% Exchanges: $^1/_2$ Starch, 1 Fat Carbohydrate Choices: $^1/_2$

come together for
kwanzaa

Aloha Tea Cakes • Praline Sugar Cookies • Handprint Cookies •
Candied Fruit Drops • Sour Cream Cherry Bars • Sweet Potato Pie
• Cranberry Peach Pie • Black Forest Tart • Quick Red Velvet Cake
• Festive Pound Cake with Fruit Compote • Cherry-Berry Cobbler
• Fresh Pear-Date Bread • Plum Pudding Bread • Queen's Muffins
• Sweet Potato Streusel Muffins • Chocolate Chip Macadamia Nut
Muffins • Double Orange Scones with Orange Butter • Tiny Ham
and Pineapple Pot Pies • Cheddar and Bacon Biscuits •
Sausage Snack Wraps

aloha tea cakes

Prep Time: **15 minutes**   Start to Finish: **45 minutes**   6 $\frac{1}{2}$ dozen cookies

TEA CAKES

1 cup coconut

1 cup granulated sugar

$^3/_4$ cup packed brown sugar

1 cup butter or margarine,
   softened

2 eggs

3 cups all-purpose flour

1 teaspoon baking powder

1 teaspoon baking soda

1 teaspoon ground allspice

$^1/_2$ teaspoon salt

$^3/_4$ to 1 cup chopped macadamia
   nuts or cashews

1 can (8 oz) crushed pineapple,
   drained, $^1/_3$ cup liquid reserved

FROSTING

4 cups powdered sugar

$^1/_2$ teaspoon salt

$^1/_4$ to 1 teaspoon ground ginger

$^1/_2$ cup butter or margarine,
   softened

$^1/_3$ cup reserved pineapple liquid

1   Heat oven to 350°F. Grease cookie sheets with shortening. Place coconut in ungreased shallow pan. Bake 4 to 6 minutes or until toasted, stirring occasionally.

2   In large bowl, beat granulated sugar, brown sugar and 1 cup butter until light and fluffy. Add eggs; mix well. By hand, stir in flour, baking powder, baking soda, allspice and salt; mix well. Stir in toasted coconut, macadamia nuts and pineapple; mix well. Drop by rounded teaspoonfuls 2 inches apart onto cookie sheets.

3   Bake 8 to 10 minutes or until light golden brown. Remove from cookie sheets; cool completely. In large bowl, beat all frosting ingredients until smooth and fluffy. Generously frost cooled cookies.

These spicy-sweet cookies are flavored

with allspice. Despite its name, allspice is just one spice. It gets its name because it tastes like a combination of cinnamon, nutmeg and cloves.

High Altitude (3500–6500 ft):
No change.

1 Cookie: Calories 110 (Calories from Fat 45); Total Fat 5g (Saturated Fat 2.5g; Trans Fat 0g); Cholesterol 15mg; Sodium 85mg; Total Carbohydrate 16g (Dietary Fiber 0g; Sugars 12g); Protein 0g % Daily Value: Vitamin A 2%; Vitamin C 0%; Calcium 0%; Iron 0% Exchanges: 1 Other Carbohydrate, 1 Fat Carbohydrate Choices: 1

praline sugar cookies

Prep Time: **1 hour 10 minutes**   Start to Finish: **1 hour 10 minutes**   26 cookies

$^1/_4$ cup granulated sugar

$^1/_4$ cup pecan halves

1 roll (16.5 oz) refrigerated sugar
   cookies

$^1/_4$ cup packed brown sugar

1 teaspoon vanilla

$^1/_3$ to $^1/_2$ cup coarse white
   sparkling sugar or granulated
   sugar

1 In 8-inch heavy skillet, melt granulated sugar over medium-low heat 6 to 8 minutes, swirling pan frequently, until golden brown. Watch carefully to avoid scorching. Remove from heat. Stir in pecans until coated. Pour mixture onto sheet of foil. Cool until hard, about 15 minutes. Finely chop pecan-sugar candy.

2 Heat oven to 325°F. In large bowl, break up cookie dough. Stir in brown sugar and vanilla until well blended. Stir in chopped pecan-sugar candy.

3 Using about 1 measuring tablespoon dough for each, shape dough into balls and roll in coarse sugar; place 2 inches apart on ungreased cookie sheets.

4 Bake 11 to 16 minutes or until edges are light golden brown. Cool 2 minutes; remove from cookie sheets.

Be sure to watch the sugar mixture carefully—it turns
a pretty golden brown when caramelized. If it gets
too brown, it will taste burned.

High Altitude (3500–6500 ft): Melt granulated sugar over medium heat 10 to 12 minutes, without stirring, until golden brown. Watch carefully to avoid scorching.

1 Cookie: Calories 110 (Calories from Fat 35); Total Fat 4g (Saturated Fat 1g; Trans Fat 1g); Cholesterol 5mg; Sodium 50mg; Total Carbohydrate 17g (Dietary Fiber 0g; Sugars 12g); Protein 0g % Daily Value: Vitamin A 0%; Vitamin C 0%; Calcium 0%; Iron 2% Exchanges: 1 Other Carbohydrate, 1 Fat Carbohydrate Choices: 1

handprint cookies

extra easy

| Prep Time: 30 minutes | Start to Finish: 1 hour | 2 dozen cookies |

1 roll (16.5 oz) refrigerated sugar cookies

Colored sugars or decorating icings and gels, if desired

1 Heat oven to 350°F. Cut well-chilled dough in half. Refrigerate remaining dough while rolling first half. Sprinkle work surface with flour; coat sides of dough with flour. Roll to $^1/_4$-inch thickness, adding flour as needed to prevent sticking.

2 Using 3- to 3 $^1/_2$-inch hand-shaped cookie cutter dipped in flour, cut hand shapes. If decorating with colored sugars, sprinkle over hand shapes. Place shapes 2 inches apart on ungreased cookie sheets. Refrigerate cutouts on cookie sheet for 15 minutes before baking to prevent the "fingers" from baking together.

3 Bake 8 to 11 minutes or until edges are light golden brown. Cool 1 minute; carefully remove from cookie sheets to cooling racks. Cool completely, about 30 minutes. Decorate as desired with sugars, icings or gels.

Created in 1966 by Dr. Maulana Karenga, a teacher and civil rights leader, "Kwanzaa" is Swahili for "first fruits of the harvest."

High Altitude (3500–6500 ft): In step 1, in large bowl, break up cookie dough. Stir or knead in $^1/_2$ cup flour. In step 3, bake 5 to 8 minutes.

1 Cookie without Decorations: Calories 80 (Calories from Fat 35); Total Fat 3.5g (Saturated Fat 1g; Trans Fat 1g); Cholesterol 5mg; Sodium 50mg; Total Carbohydrate 12g (Dietary Fiber 0g; Sugars 6g); Protein 0g % Daily Value: Vitamin A 0%; Vitamin C 0%; Calcium 0%; Iron 2% Exchanges: $^1/_2$ Other Carbohydrate, 1 Fat Carbohydrate Choices: 1

kwanzaa cutouts

This seven-day holiday (beginning on December 26) is a celebration of family, culture and community, especially enjoyed by children. Gather friends and family to make these colorful cookies decorated in the Kwanzaa colors of red, green and black.

Let kids look through magazines for pictures of African fabric and designs to make invitations and party decorations using those designs.

Celebrate the harvest theme with fruit- and vegetable-shaped cookies frosted and decorated in a rainbow of colors.

Create a hands of unity cookie wreath! On large flat serving plate, arrange Handprint Cookies slightly overlapping with fingers pointed out in wreath.

Cut seven candle shapes to make a cookie candelabrum and arrange on large flat serving platter; put a small yellow or orange candy at the top of each for "flame."

candied fruit drops

Prep Time: **1 hour 15 minutes**   Start to Finish: **1 hour 15 minutes**   7 dozen cookies

1 cup butter or margarine,
   softened

³/₄ cup packed brown sugar

1 egg

1 ³/₄ cups all-purpose flour

¹/₂ teaspoon baking soda

¹/₂ teaspoon salt

1 box (8 oz) chopped dates (1 ¹/₂
   cups)

1 cup chopped candied green
   pineapple

1 cup chopped candied red
   cherries

1 ¹/₂ cups chopped pecans

1 Heat oven to 350°F. In large bowl, beat butter and brown sugar until light and fluffy. Add egg; blend well. Add flour, baking soda and salt; mix well. Stir in dates, candied fruit and pecans. Drop by teaspoonfuls onto ungreased cookie sheets.

2 Bake 10 to 12 minutes. Cool 1 minute; remove from cookie sheets. Cool completely.

Dates and candied fruit make these drop cookies wink at you with color, and they're very chewy and moist!

High Altitude (3500–6500 ft):
Increase flour to 2 cups.

1 Cookie: Calories 70 (Calories from Fat 35); Total Fat 3.5g (Saturated Fat 1.5g; Trans Fat 0g); Cholesterol 10mg; Sodium 45mg; Total Carbohydrate 10g (Dietary Fiber 0g; Sugars 6g); Protein 0g % Daily Value: Vitamin A 0%; Vitamin C 0%; Calcium 0%; Iron 0% Exchanges: ¹/₂ Other Carbohydrate, 1 Fat Carbohydrate Choices: ¹/₂

sour cream cherry bars

Prep Time: **15 minutes**   Start to Finish: **2 hours 30 minutes**   60 bars

BASE AND TOPPING

1 cup packed brown sugar

1 cup butter or margarine,
    softened

2 cups quick-cooking oats

1 ^{1}/$_2$ cups all-purpose flour

1 teaspoon baking soda

FILLING

^{3}/$_4$ cup granulated sugar

^{1}/$_4$ cup all-purpose flour

1 tablespoon grated orange peel

1 cup sour cream

1 teaspoon almond extract

1 egg

4 ^{1}/$_2$ cups frozen pitted tart
    cherries, thawed (24 oz)

1 Heat oven to 350°F. In large bowl, blend brown sugar and butter. Add oats, 1 ^{1}/$_2$ cups flour and the baking soda; mix until crumbs form. Press half of crumb mixture in bottom of ungreased 15 × 10 × 1-inch pan; reserve remaining mixture for topping. Bake 10 minutes.

2 Meanwhile, in large bowl, mix all filling ingredients except cherries. Stir in cherries.

3 Pour filling over partially baked crust. Crumble and sprinkle remaining half of crumb mixture over filling.

4 Bake 25 to 35 minutes longer or until center is set. Cool completely, about 1 ^{1}/$_2$ hours. For bars, cut into 10 rows by 6 rows. Store in refrigerator.

Pure comfort! Buttery and brown sugary, these old-fashioned bars will be a sure hit. Pack the bars in a decorative container for a tasty gift.

High Altitude (3500–6500 ft):
No change.

1 Bar: Calories 90 (Calories from Fat 35); Total Fat 4g (Saturated Fat 2.5g; Trans Fat 0g); Cholesterol 15mg; Sodium 45mg; Total Carbohydrate 13g (Dietary Fiber 0g; Sugars 8g); Protein 1g % Daily Value: Vitamin A 2%; Vitamin C 0%; Calcium 0%; Iron 2% Exchanges: ^{1}/$_2$ Starch, ^{1}/$_2$ Other Carbohydrate, ^{1}/$_2$ Fat Carbohydrate Choices: 1

sweet potato pie

Prep Time: **30 minutes**   Start to Finish: **2 hours 30 minutes**   8 servings

CRUST

1 refrigerated pie crust (from 15-oz box), softened as directed on box

FILLING

1 $^1/_2$ cups mashed cooked dark orange sweet potatoes (1 medium; about 1 lb)

2 cups sugar

1 to 2 tablespoons ground cinnamon

2 to 3 teaspoons ground nutmeg

$^1/_2$ to $^3/_4$ teaspoon ground cloves

$^1/_2$ to $^3/_4$ teaspoon ground mace

$^1/_4$ to $^1/_2$ teaspoon ground ginger

$^1/_2$ cup butter or margarine, melted

3 tablespoons vanilla

3 eggs, slightly beaten

$^1/_3$ cup evaporated milk

1 Heat oven to 350°F. Make pie crust as directed on box for One-Crust Filled Pie using 9-inch glass pie plate.

2 In large bowl, beat sweet potatoes, sugar, cinnamon, nutmeg, cloves, mace, ginger and butter with electric mixer on low speed 1 to 2 minutes or until well blended. Add vanilla, eggs and milk; blend well. Pour into crust-lined pan.

3 Bake 20 to 30 minutes; cover edge of crust with strips of foil to prevent excessive browning. Bake 30 minutes longer or until filling is set. Cool completely. Store in refrigerator.

Sweet potato pie recipes are often handed down from generation to generation, and everyone has a favorite version. Give this recipe a try—it's rich with extra butter and has lots of spices!

High Altitude (3500–6500 ft): In step 3, increase first bake time to 25 to 35 minutes.

1 Serving: Calories 550 (Calories from Fat 190); Total Fat 21g (Saturated Fat 11g; Trans Fat 0.5g); Cholesterol 115mg; Sodium 260mg; Total Carbohydrate 82g (Dietary Fiber 3g; Sugars 58g); Protein 5g % Daily Value: Vitamin A 310%; Vitamin C 15%; Calcium 8%; Iron 6% Exchanges: 1 $^1/_2$ Starch, 4 Other Carbohydrate, 4 Fat Carbohydrate Choices: 5 $^1/_2$

cranberry peach pie

| Prep Time: **40 minutes** | Start to Finish: **1 hour 20 minutes** | 8 servings |

CRUST

1 box (15 oz) refrigerated pie
   crusts, softened as directed
   on box

FILLING

2 cups fresh or frozen
   cranberries

$^1/_2$ cup sugar

2 tablespoons cornstarch

1 can (21 oz) peach pie filling
   with more fruit

1 egg yolk, beaten

1 teaspoon water

Easy as pie! Refrigerated pie
crust and peach pie filling
make this pie easy. Use any
of your favorite cookie or
canapé cutters to make the
pie crust cutouts.

1 Heat oven to 425°F. Place pie crust in 9-inch glass pie plate as directed on box for One-Crust Filled Pie.

2 In large bowl, mix cranberries, sugar and cornstarch. Add pie filling; stir gently. Spoon into crust-lined pan.

3 Unroll second pie crust on work surface. Use star-shaped canapé or cookie cutter to cut pattern of stars in dough, cutting to within 1 $^1/_2$ inches of edge. Reserve cutouts. Place crust over filling; fold edge of top crust under bottom crust. Press together to seal.

4 Dip fork tines in flour; press fork tines diagonally on edge of dough. Rotate tines 90 degrees and press next to first set of marks. Continue this back-and-forth pattern around rim.

5 In small bowl, mix egg yolk and water; gently brush over top crust. Arrange star cutouts on top crust; brush with egg yolk mixture.

6 Bake 15 to 20 minutes; cover edge of crust with strips of foil to prevent excessive browning. Bake 15 to 20 minutes longer or until crust is deep golden brown and filling is bubbly.

High Altitude (3500–6500 ft): In step 6, increase second bake time to 20 to 25 minutes.

1 Serving: Calories 380 (Calories from Fat 130); Total Fat 15g (Saturated Fat 5g; Trans Fat 0g); Cholesterol 35mg; Sodium 220mg; Total Carbohydrate 61g (Dietary Fiber 2g; Sugars 28g); Protein 0g % Daily Value: Vitamin A 0%; Vitamin C 4%; Calcium 0%; Iron 0% Exchanges: $^1/_2$ Starch, 3 $^1/_2$ Other Carbohydrate, 3 Fat Carbohydrate Choices: 4

black forest tart

Prep Time: **30 minutes**   Start to Finish: **2 hours 30 minutes**   12 servings

CRUST

1 refrigerated pie crust (from 15-
oz box), softened as directed
on box

FILLING

6 oz semisweet baking
chocolate, cut into pieces

2 tablespoons butter or
margarine

$^1/_4$ cup powdered sugar

1 package (8 oz) cream cheese,
softened

1 can (21 oz) cherry pie filling
with more fruit

TOPPING

1 cup whipping cream, whipped

1 oz semisweet baking
chocolate, grated

1 Heat oven to 450°F. Place pie crust in 9-inch pie pan or 10-inch tart pan with removable bottom as directed on box for One-Crust Filled Pie. Bake 9 to 11 minutes or until lightly browned. Cool.

2 In small saucepan, melt 6 oz chocolate and the butter over low heat, stirring constantly; remove from heat. In small bowl, beat powdered sugar and cream cheese. Stir in melted chocolate mixture; beat until smooth. Add 1 cup of the cherry pie filling; blend gently. Set aside remaining pie filling. Spread mixture evenly into cooled crust. Refrigerate 1 hour.

3 In small bowl, mix topping ingredients. Spread evenly over cooled chocolate layer. Spoon remaining cherry pie filling in a band around outer edge of tart. Refrigerate until serving time.

Make this impressive chocolate-cherry tart up to 24 hours ahead of time and store covered in the fridge. Instead of using grated chocolate, garnish the top of the pie with whipped cream and chocolate curls. Or, garnish each slice with a dollop of whipped cream and a well-drained, stemmed maraschino cherry or a chocolate-covered cherry!

High Altitude (3500–6500 ft):
No change.

1 Serving: Calories 370 (Calories from Fat 220); Total Fat 24g (Saturated Fat 14g; Trans Fat 0g); Cholesterol 50mg; Sodium 150mg; Total Carbohydrate 35g (Dietary Fiber 2g; Sugars 23g); Protein 3g % Daily Value: Vitamin A 10%; Vitamin C 2%; Calcium 4%; Iron 6% Exchanges: 1 Starch, 1 $^1/_2$ Other Carbohydrate, 4 $^1/_2$ Fat Carbohydrate Choices: 2

quick red velvet cake

Prep Time: **40 minutes**   Start to Finish: **2 hours 45 minutes**   16 servings

CAKE

1 box (1 lb 2.25 oz) devil's food
   cake mix with pudding

1 cup sour cream

1/2 cup water

1/4 cup vegetable oil

1 bottle (1 oz) red food color

3 eggs

FROSTING

1/2 cup all-purpose flour

1 1/2 cups milk

1 1/2 cups sugar

1 1/2 cups butter or margarine,
   softened

1 tablespoon vanilla

1 Heat oven to 350°F (if using dark or nonstick pans, heat oven to 325°F). Grease two 9-inch round cake pans with shortening. In large bowl, beat all cake ingredients with electric mixer on low speed 30 seconds or until moistened. Beat on medium speed 2 minutes, scraping bowl occasionally. Pour batter into pans.

2 Bake 25 to 35 minutes or until top springs back when touched lightly in center. Cool 15 minutes. Remove from pans; cool completely.

3 Meanwhile, in medium saucepan, cook flour and milk over medium heat, stirring constantly, until mixture is very thick. Cover surface with plastic wrap; cool to room temperature.

4 In large bowl, beat sugar and butter until light and fluffy. Gradually add flour mixture by tablespoonfuls, beating with electric mixer on high speed until smooth. Beat in vanilla.

5 Place 1 cake layer, top side down, on serving plate; spread with 1 cup frosting. Top with second layer, top side up. Frost side and top of cake with frosting. Store in refrigerator.

Cake mix makes this favorite very easy, but everyone knows it's the frosting that makes this cake fabulous—and that's still made from scratch. Enjoy the cake with flavored coffees like amaretto or hazelnut.

High Altitude (3500–6500 ft):
No change.

1 Serving: Calories 460 (Calories from Fat 240); Total Fat 27g (Saturated Fat 15g; Trans Fat 1.5g); Cholesterol 95mg; Sodium 400mg; Total Carbohydrate 50g (Dietary Fiber 0g; Sugars 36g); Protein 4g % Daily Value: Vitamin A 15%; Vitamin C 0%; Calcium 8%; Iron 8% Exchanges: 1 Starch, 2 1/2 Other Carbohydrate, 5 Fat Carbohydrate Choices: 3

festive pound cake with fruit compote

| Prep Time: **45 minutes** | Start to Finish: **3 hours 35 minutes** | *16 servings* |

CAKE

2 ¹/₂ cups sugar

1 ¹/₂ cups butter or margarine, softened

1 teaspoon vanilla

6 eggs

3 cups all-purpose flour

¹/₂ teaspoon baking powder

¹/₂ teaspoon salt

2 tablespoons grated orange peel

¹/₂ cup milk

COMPOTE

³/₄ cup cut-up dried apricots

1 package (3.5 oz) sweetened dried cherries (²/₃ cup)

¹/₂ cup sugar

³/₄ cup orange juice

1 tablespoon brandy

1 medium orange, peeled, chopped (about 1 cup)

Ice cream, if desired

1 Heat oven to 350°F. Generously grease 10-inch angel food (tube cake) pan with shortening; lightly flour. In large bowl, beat 2 ¹/₂ cups sugar and the butter until light and fluffy. Add vanilla; mix well. Beat in 1 egg at a time until well blended.

2 In small bowl, mix flour, baking powder and salt. Add flour mixture alternately with orange peel and milk, beating well after each addition. Pour batter into pan.

3 Bake 55 to 65 minutes or until toothpick inserted in center comes out clean. Cool 15 minutes. Invert cake onto serving plate. Cool completely, about 1 ¹/₂ hours.

4 In medium saucepan, mix apricots, cherries, ¹/₂ cup sugar and the orange juice. Heat to boiling; simmer 10 to 15 minutes or until most of liquid is absorbed. Stir in brandy and chopped orange. Serve warm compote with cake and ice cream.

Dried cherries are delicious, but can be a bit difficult to find and are a little pricey; if you can't find them, substitute cherry-flavored dried cranberries.

High Altitude (3500–6500 ft): Decrease sugar in cake to 2 ¹/₄ cups.

1 Serving: Calories 470 (Calories from Fat 180); Total Fat 20g (Saturated Fat 12g; Trans Fat 1g); Cholesterol 125mg; Sodium 240mg; Total Carbohydrate 68g (Dietary Fiber 2g; Sugars 47g); Protein 6g % Daily Value: Vitamin A 20%; Vitamin C 10%; Calcium 4%; Iron 10% Exchanges: 1 ¹/₂ Starch, 3 Other Carbohydrate, 4 Fat Carbohydrate Choices: 4 ¹/₂

cherry-berry cobbler

Prep Time: **25 minutes**   Start to Finish: **1 hour 10 minutes**   8 servings

1 bag (16 oz) frozen pitted tart
  cherries
1 bag (14 oz) frozen mixed
  berries
2 cups sugar
$1/4$ cup cornstarch
2 tablespoons water
1 egg white
$1/2$ cup sliced almonds
2 teaspoons ground cinnamon
1 can (12 oz) refrigerated
  buttermilk flaky biscuits
Ice cream, if desired

1 Heat oven to 375°F. Spray 13 × 9-inch (3-quart) glass baking dish with cooking spray. In large saucepan, mix cherries, berries, 1 $1/2$ cups of the sugar, the cornstarch and water. Cook over medium-high heat, stirring frequently, until mixture boils and thickens. Pour into baking dish.

2 In medium bowl, beat egg white until frothy. In another medium bowl, mix remaining $1/2$ cup sugar, the almonds and cinnamon.

3 Separate dough into 10 biscuits. Cut each into quarters. Dip dough pieces in egg white; toss in sugar-almond mixture to coat. Arrange on hot fruit mixture. Sprinkle any remaining sugar-almond mixture over top.

4 Bake 20 to 25 minutes or until biscuits are deep golden brown and no longer doughy in center. Let stand 20 minutes before serving. Serve warm cobbler with ice cream.

Many stores carry both sweet cherries and tart pie cherries. Bags marked just "cherries" are the tart variety typically used in pies. The fruit mixture must be piping hot when you arrange the dough pieces; that starts the baking process to cook the biscuits all the way through.

High Altitude (3500–6500 ft):
In step 4, bake 25 to 30 minutes.

1 Serving: Calories 490 (Calories from Fat 80); Total Fat 9g (Saturated Fat 1.5g; Trans Fat 2g); Cholesterol 0mg; Sodium 460mg; Total Carbohydrate 98g (Dietary Fiber 3g; Sugars 73g); Protein 5g % Daily Value: Vitamin A 0%; Vitamin C 20%; Calcium 4%; Iron 10% Exchanges: 1 $1/2$ Starch, 1 Fruit, 4 Other Carbohydrate, 1 $1/2$ Fat Carbohydrate Choices: 6 $1/2$

fresh pear-date bread

Prep Time: **10 minutes**   Start to Finish: **2 hours 40 minutes**   1 loaf (16 slices)

1 box (16.6 oz) date quick bread
   & muffin mix*

1 cup water

2 tablespoons vegetable oil

1 egg

³/₄ cup chopped peeled pear

1 ¹/₂ teaspoons grated
   lemon peel

1 Heat oven to 350°F. Grease bottom only of 8 × 4- or 9 × 5-inch loaf pan with shortening; lightly flour. In large bowl, stir quick bread mix, water, oil and egg 50 to 75 strokes with spoon until mix is moistened. Stir in pear and lemon peel. Pour batter into pan.

2 Bake 50 to 60 minutes or until toothpick inserted in center comes out clean. Cool in pan on cooling rack 15 minutes. Remove from pan. Cool completely, about 1 hour 15 minutes. Wrap tightly; store in refrigerator.

*Cranberry or nut quick bread & muffin mix can be used instead.

For a holiday gift, wrap the bread in colored foil or plastic wrap and tie it with a pretty ribbon.

High Altitude (3500–6500 ft): Heat oven to 375°F. Add 1 tablespoon all-purpose flour to dry quick bread & muffin mix. Bake 40 to 50 minutes.

1 Slice: Calories 140 (Calories from Fat 30); Total Fat 3.5g (Saturated Fat 0g; Trans Fat 0g); Cholesterol 15mg; Sodium 105mg; Total Carbohydrate 25g (Dietary Fiber 1g; Sugars 14g); Protein 2g % Daily Value: Vitamin A 0%; Vitamin C 0%; Calcium 0%; Iron 4% Exchanges: 1 Starch, ¹/₂ Other Carbohydrate, ¹/₂ Fat Carbohydrate Choices: 1 ¹/₂

plum pudding bread

| Prep Time: **15 minutes** | Start to Finish: **1 hour 40 minutes** | 12 servings |

1 can (16.5 oz) purple plums in
   syrup, drained, $^1/_2$ cup syrup
   reserved and plums pitted
1 box (16.6 oz) date quick bread
   & muffin mix*
$^1/_2$ teaspoon ground ginger
$^1/_2$ teaspoon ground cinnamon
$^1/_4$ teaspoon ground nutmeg
2 tablespoons vegetable oil
1 egg

1 Heat oven to 350°F. Grease 8- or 9-inch springform pan. In food processor bowl with metal blade, place plums. Cover; process until smooth.

2 In medium bowl, stir quick bread mix, pureed plums, reserved $^1/_2$ cup plum liquid, ginger, cinnamon, nutmeg, oil and egg just until dry ingredients are moistened. Pour batter into pan.

3 Bake 40 to 50 minutes or until toothpick inserted in center comes out clean. Cool in pan 10 minutes. Remove side of pan. Cool 25 minutes.

*Cranberry or nut quick bread & muffin mix can be used instead.

Traditionally, plum pudding is a steamed Christmas dessert, made with spices, fruits, nuts and bread crumbs. This bread is reminiscent of the traditional dessert. For a special spread, blend $^1/_4$ cup plum jam and $^1/_3$ to $^1/_2$ cup softened butter. Serve it with the warm bread.

High Altitude (3500–6500 ft): Add 2 tablespoons all-purpose flour to dry quick bread & muffin mix.

1 Serving: Calories 220 (Calories from Fat 40); Total Fat 4.5g (Saturated Fat 0g; Trans Fat 0g); Cholesterol 20mg; Sodium 140mg; Total Carbohydrate 41g (Dietary Fiber 2g; Sugars 25g); Protein 3g % Daily Value: Vitamin A 2%; Vitamin C 0%; Calcium 0%; Iron 6% Exchanges: 1 Starch, 1 $^1/_2$ Other Carbohydrate, 1 Fat Carbohydrate Choices: 3

queen's muffins

Prep Time: **20 minutes**   Start to Finish: **55 minutes**   18 muffins

1 cup granulated sugar

1 cup butter or margarine, softened

3 eggs

1 teaspoon lemon extract

1 teaspoon orange extract

2 cups all-purpose flour

2 teaspoons baking powder

$^1/_2$ teaspoon ground cinnamon

1 box (10 oz) dried currants

2 tablespoons powdered sugar

1 Heat oven to 325°F. Place paper baking cup in each of 18 regular-size muffin cups. In large bowl, beat granulated sugar and butter until light and fluffy. Beat in 1 egg at a time until well blended. Add lemon and orange extracts; beat well.

2 Gradually add flour, baking powder and cinnamon; mix well. Stir in currants. Pour batter into muffin cups, filling each $^3/_4$ full.

3 Bake 25 to 30 minutes or until toothpick inserted in center comes out clean. Immediately remove from pan; cool 5 minutes. Sprinkle with powdered sugar.

In Colonial America, it was common for cake to be named after the rank of royalty. The cost of the ingredients for a cake was related to the importance of rank. For example, King's Cake called for expensive fruits, nuts and spices. The next most expensive cake was Queen's Cake, made with fruits, spices and brandy. This version of Queen's Cake is a very rich butter muffin filled with currants, cinnamon and citrus flavorings.

High Altitude (3500–6500 ft): Increase flour to 2 $^1/_4$ cups.

1 Muffin: Calories 260 (Calories from Fat 100); Total Fat 11g (Saturated Fat 7g; Trans Fat 0.5g); Cholesterol 60mg; Sodium 140mg; Total Carbohydrate 35g (Dietary Fiber 2g; Sugars 23g); Protein 3g % Daily Value: Vitamin A 8%; Vitamin C 0%; Calcium 6%; Iron 8% Exchanges: 1 Starch, 1 $^1/_2$ Other Carbohydrate, 2 Fat Carbohydrate Choices: 2

sweet potato streusel muffins

Prep Time: **25 minutes**   Start to Finish: **45 minutes**   15 muffins

MUFFINS

1 ¹/₂ cups all-purpose flour

³/₄ cup cornmeal

¹/₂ cup granulated sugar

¹/₄ cup chopped peanuts

¹/₄ cup golden raisins

3 teaspoons baking powder

1 teaspoon ground nutmeg

2 eggs

1 cup mashed cooked sweet
  potato (1 small to medium;
  about 10 to 12 oz)

²/₃ cup milk

2 tablespoons vegetable oil

TOPPING

3 tablespoons packed brown
  sugar

2 tablespoons chopped peanuts

1 tablespoon butter or
  margarine, softened

1 Heat oven to 400°F. Spray 15 regular-size muffin cups with cooking spray. In medium bowl, mix flour, cornmeal, granulated sugar, ¹/₄ cup peanuts, the raisins, baking powder and nutmeg.

2 In medium bowl, beat eggs slightly. Add sweet potato, milk and oil; blend well. Add to dry ingredients all at once; stir just until dry particles are moistened. (Batter will be lumpy.) Fill muffin cups ²/₃ full.

3 In small bowl, mix all topping ingredients. Sprinkle evenly over muffins.

4 Bake 15 to 20 minutes or until toothpick inserted in center comes out clean. Serve warm.

M-m-m, sweetly spiced muffins made oh-so-moist with sweet potatoes! If you like, substitute canned pumpkin (not pumpkin pie mix) for the sweet potato. For an indulgent dessert or treat, split the muffins in half and spread with cream cheese frosting.

High Altitude (3500–6500 ft):
No change.

1 Muffin: Calories 190 (Calories from Fat 50); Total Fat 6g (Saturated Fat 1.5g; Trans Fat 0g); Cholesterol 30mg; Sodium 135mg; Total Carbohydrate 31g (Dietary Fiber 2g; Sugars 13g); Protein 5g % Daily Value: Vitamin A 70%; Vitamin C 2%; Calcium 8%; Iron 8% Exchanges: 1 Starch, 1 Other Carbohydrate, 1 Fat Carbohydrate Choices: 2

chocolate chip macadamia nut muffins

| Prep Time: **15 minutes** | Start to Finish: **35 minutes** | 18 muffins |

STREUSEL

$^{1}/_{4}$ cup all-purpose flour

$^{1}/_{4}$ cup packed brown sugar

2 tablespoons butter or
   margarine

MUFFINS

2 cups all-purpose flour

$^{1}/_{2}$ cup granulated sugar

1 teaspoon baking powder

$^{1}/_{2}$ teaspoon baking soda

$^{1}/_{2}$ teaspoon salt

$^{3}/_{4}$ cup sour cream

$^{1}/_{2}$ cup butter or margarine,
   melted

$^{1}/_{4}$ cup milk

1 tablespoon vanilla

1 egg

$^{1}/_{2}$ cup chopped macadamia nuts

$^{1}/_{2}$ cup miniature semisweet
   chocolate chips

1 Heat oven to 375°F. Grease 18 regular-size muffin cups or place paper baking cup in each muffin cup. In small bowl, mix all streusel ingredients with fork until mixture resembles coarse crumbs. Set aside.

2 In large bowl, mix 2 cups flour, the granulated sugar, baking powder, baking soda and salt. Add sour cream, $^{1}/_{2}$ cup butter, the milk, vanilla and egg; stir just until dry particles are moistened. Fold in macadamia nuts and chocolate chips. Fill muffin cups $^{3}/_{4}$ full; sprinkle each with 1 $^{1}/_{2}$ teaspoons streusel.

3 Bake 18 to 20 minutes or until toothpick inserted in center comes out clean. Remove from muffin cups immediately. Serve warm.

Serve these muffins warm from the oven with tea or coffee.

High Altitude (3500–6500 ft): Increase flour in muffins by 2 tablespoons.

1 Muffin: Calories 220 (Calories from Fat 110); Total Fat 12g (Saturated Fat 7g; Trans Fat 0g); Cholesterol 35mg; Sodium 190mg; Total Carbohydrate 25g (Dietary Fiber 1g; Sugars 12g); Protein 3g % Daily Value: Vitamin A 6%; Vitamin C 0%; Calcium 4%; Iron 6% Exchanges: 1 Starch, $^{1}/_{2}$ Other Carbohydrate, 2 $^{1}/_{2}$ Fat Carbohydrate Choices: 1 $^{1}/_{2}$

double orange scones with orange butter

Prep Time: **15 minutes**	Start to Finish: **35 minutes**	8 scones

SCONES

2 cups all-purpose flour

3 tablespoons sugar

2 $1/2$ teaspoons baking powder

2 teaspoons grated orange peel

$1/3$ cup butter or margarine

$1/2$ cup chopped mandarin
orange segments, drained
(from 11 oz-can)

$1/4$ cup milk

1 egg, slightly beaten

1 tablespoon sugar

ORANGE BUTTER

$1/2$ cup butter or margarine,
softened

2 tablespoons orange marmalade

1 Heat oven to 400°F. Lightly grease cookie sheet with shortening. In large bowl, mix flour, 3 tablespoons sugar, the baking powder and orange peel. With fork or pastry blender, cut in $1/3$ cup butter until mixture resembles coarse crumbs. Add orange segments, milk and egg. With fork, stir just until mixture leaves sides of bowl and soft dough forms.

2 Turn dough out onto floured surface. Knead lightly 10 times. On cookie sheet, roll or pat dough into 6-inch circle. Sprinkle with 1 tablespoon sugar. Cut into 8 wedges; separate slightly.

3 Bake 15 to 20 minutes or until golden brown.

4 In small bowl, beat $1/2$ cup butter until light and fluffy; stir in marmalade. Serve with warm scones.

Rich, tender scones are made extra moist with bits of mandarin oranges. They are doubly delicious served warm with Orange Butter—have the girls over for a cup of coffee!

High Altitude (3500–6500 ft):
Increase flour to 2 $1/4$ cups.

1 Scone: Calories 340 (Calories from Fat 180); Total Fat 20g (Saturated Fat 13g; Trans Fat 1g); Cholesterol 80mg; Sodium 300mg; Total Carbohydrate 36g (Dietary Fiber 1g; Sugars 10g); Protein 5g % Daily Value: Vitamin A 15%; Vitamin C 4%; Calcium 10%; Iron 10% Exchanges: 1 Starch, 1 $1/2$ Other Carbohydrate, 4 Fat Carbohydrate Choices: 2 $1/2$

tiny ham and pineapple pot pies

Prep Time: **40 minutes**	Start to Finish: **1 hour**	16 appetizers

$^{1}/_{2}$ cup finely chopped cooked ham

$^{1}/_{2}$ cup finely shredded Swiss cheese (2 oz)

$^{1}/_{2}$ cup well-drained canned crushed pineapple

1 tablespoon finely chopped green onion (1 medium)

$^{1}/_{2}$ teaspoon ground mustard

1 box (15 oz) refrigerated pie crusts, softened as directed on box

1 egg, beaten

1 teaspoon sesame seed, if desired

1 Heat oven to 450°F (if using dark or nonstick pans, heat oven to 425°F). In small bowl, mix ham, cheese, pineapple, onion and mustard.

2 Remove crusts from pouches; unroll on work surface. From each crust, cut eight 3-inch rounds and eight 2-inch rounds, rerolling crusts if necessary. Press 3-inch rounds in bottoms and up sides of 16 ungreased mini muffin cups so edges of crusts extend slightly over sides of cups.

3 Spoon about 1 rounded tablespoon ham mixture into each crust-lined cup. Brush edges of crust lightly with beaten egg.

4 Cut small vent in each 2-inch pie-crust round. Place 1 round over filling in each cup; press edges together, pushing toward cup so crust does not extend over sides. Brush tops with beaten egg. Sprinkle with sesame seed.

5 Bake 10 to 14 minutes or until crust is deep golden brown. Remove from muffin cups. Let stand 5 minutes before serving.

These pot pies are perfect for a holiday buffet or cocktail party. Fill, top, cover and refrigerate the pot pies up to 2 hours ahead. Just before baking, brush the tops with egg and sprinkle with sesame seed.

High Altitude (3500–6500 ft): No change.

1 Appetizer: Calories 120 (Calories from Fat 60); Total Fat 7g (Saturated Fat 2.5g; Trans Fat 0g); Cholesterol 20mg; Sodium 150mg; Total Carbohydrate 11g (Dietary Fiber 0g; Sugars 1g); Protein 2g % Daily Value: Vitamin A 0%; Vitamin C 0%; Calcium 4%; Iron 0% Exchanges: $^{1}/_{2}$ Starch, 1 $^{1}/_{2}$ Fat Carbohydrate Choices: 1

cheddar and bacon biscuits

extra
easy

Prep Time: **5 minutes**	Start to Finish: **30 minutes**	4 biscuits

4 frozen buttermilk biscuits
(from 25-oz bag)

2 teaspoons cooked real bacon
pieces (from 3-oz jar or
package)

2 tablespoons finely shredded
Cheddar cheese

1 Heat oven to 375°F. Place frozen biscuits on ungreased cookie sheet, sides touching. Bake 10 minutes.

2 Top biscuits with bacon and cheese. Bake 10 to 14 minutes longer or until golden brown. Serve warm.

Using individually frozen biscuits lets you make exactly how many you want. They would go well with just about any of your favorite suppers. Can't get any easier than this!

High Altitude (3500–6500 ft):
No change.

1 Biscuit: Calories 200 (Calories from Fat 90); Total Fat 11g (Saturated Fat 3.5g; Trans Fat 4g); Cholesterol 0mg; Sodium 620mg; Total Carbohydrate 22g (Dietary Fiber 0g; Sugars 3g); Protein 5g % Daily Value: Vitamin A 0%; Vitamin C 0%; Calcium 0%; Iron 6% Exchanges: 1 1/2 Starch, 2 Fat Carbohydrate Choices: 1 1/2

sausage snack wraps

| Prep Time: **15 minutes** | Start to Finish: **30 minutes** | 48 appetizers |

2 cans (8 oz each) refrigerated crescent dinner rolls

1 package (1 lb) cocktail-size smoked link sausages (48 sausages)

Ketchup, if desired

Prepared horseradish, if desired

Yellow mustard, if desired

1 Heat oven to 375°F. Unroll dough and separate into 16 triangles. Cut each triangle into thirds lengthwise. Place sausage on shortest side of each triangle. Roll up, starting at shortest side and rolling to opposite point. Place point side down on ungreased cookie sheet.

2 Bake 12 to 15 minutes or until golden brown. Serve warm with ketchup, horseradish and mustard.

To make these party favorites ahead, assemble them, then cover and refrigerate up to 2 hours; bake as directed. Beware—keep the food thieves out of the kitchen while you're baking these or you might not have enough left for your company!

High Altitude (3500–6500 ft):
No change.

1 Appetizer: Calories 70 (Calories from Fat 45); Total Fat 5g (Saturated Fat 1.5g; Trans Fat 0.5g); Cholesterol 5mg; Sodium 190mg; Total Carbohydrate 4g (Dietary Fiber 0g; Sugars 0g); Protein 2g % Daily Value: Vitamin A 0%; Vitamin C 0%; Calcium 0%; Iron 0% Exchanges: $^{1}/_{2}$ Starch, 1 Fat Carbohydrate Choices: 0

happy new year

Lemon-Ginger Shortbread • White Chocolate–Cashew Pretzel Bars • Pistachio Bars • Cookie Tartlets • Peppermint Whoopie Pies • Tin Roof Fudge Tart • Chocolate Silk Raspberry Tart • Coconut-Lemon Cream Tartlets • Raspberry Mirror Cake • Rich and Easy Tiramisu Dessert • Tres Leches Cake • Key Lime Cream Torte • Strawberry Brownie Mousse Torte • Chocolate Cheesecake • Banana-Eggnog Bread Pudding with Rum Sauce • Apple-Raspberry Cookie Cobbler • Pineapple-Cherry Quick Bread • Mushroom-Garlic Cream Tartlets • Crescent-Crab Purses • Mini Chicken Caesar Cups

lemon-ginger shortbread

Prep Time: **30 minutes**   Start to Finish: **1 hour 20 minutes**   32 cookies

COOKIES

1 cup butter or margarine,
    softened

$^1/_3$ cup granulated sugar

2 cups all-purpose flour

$^1/_3$ cup finely chopped
    crystallized ginger

1 tablespoon grated lemon peel

GLAZE

$^1/_2$ cup powdered sugar

2 to 4 teaspoons fresh
    lemon juice

1 Heat oven to 325°F. In large bowl, beat butter and granulated sugar until light and fluffy.

2 Add flour, ginger and lemon peel; mix well. Shape dough into ball; divide into 4 pieces. On ungreased cookie sheets, flatten each piece to 6-inch round; press edges to smooth.

3 Bake 15 to 25 minutes or until edges are light golden brown. Cool 5 minutes. Cut each round into 8 wedges; pierce surface with fork if desired. Cool completely on cookie sheet, about 15 minutes.

4 In small bowl, blend powdered sugar and enough lemon juice for desired drizzling consistency until smooth. Place mixture in small resealable food-storage plastic bag; seal bag. Cut off small corner of bag. Squeeze glaze onto cooled cookies.

Crystallized ginger is fresh peeled gingerroot that is simmered in sugar syrup, then dipped in granulated sugar and dried. Look for it in the produce department, or in jars in the spice section. It gets a little sticky during chopping, so it helps to spray your knife with cooking spray as often as needed.

High Altitude (3500–6500 ft): Increase flour to 2 $^1/_3$ cups.

1 Cookie: Calories 100 (Calories from Fat 50); Total Fat 6g (Saturated Fat 3.5g; Trans Fat 0g); Cholesterol 15mg; Sodium 45mg; Total Carbohydrate 11g (Dietary Fiber 0g; Sugars 5g); Protein 0g % Daily Value: Vitamin A 4%; Vitamin C 0%; Calcium 0%; Iron 2% Exchanges: 1 Other Carbohydrate, 1 Fat Carbohydrate Choices: 1

white chocolate–cashew pretzel bars

| Prep Time: **25 minutes** | Start to Finish: **1 hour 30 minutes** | 36 bars |

1 roll (16.5 oz) refrigerated sugar cookies

1 bag (12 oz) white chocolate chunks or white vanilla baking chips

1 cup coarsely chopped pretzel sticks or twists

1 1/2 cups semisweet chocolate chips

1/4 cup peanut butter

1 cup chopped cashews

Just how many goodies can you get into one little bar? Lots, that's why every time these show up in our test kitchens they disappear quickly! Dry-roasted peanuts are an option instead of the cashews.

1 Heat oven to 350°F. Spray 13 × 9-inch pan with cooking spray. Break up cookie dough into pan. With floured fingers, press dough evenly in bottom of pan to form crust. Sprinkle 1 cup of the white chocolate chunks and the pretzels over dough; press lightly into dough.

2 Bake 16 to 20 minutes or until light golden brown. Cool completely, about 30 minutes.

3 In small microwavable bowl, place 1/4 cup of the white chocolate chunks; set aside. In large microwavable bowl, microwave chocolate chips and remaining white chocolate chunks on High 2 minutes, stirring every 30 seconds, until melted and smooth. If necessary, microwave 30 seconds longer. Stir in peanut butter and cashews. Spread mixture evenly over cooled baked crust. Refrigerate 15 minutes to set chocolate.

4 Microwave reserved 1/4 cup white chocolate chunks on High 30 seconds; stir until melted and smooth. If necessary, microwave 10 seconds longer. Drizzle over bars. Let stand until set, about 10 minutes. For bars, cut into 6 rows by 6 rows.

High Altitude (3500–6500 ft): No change.

1 Bar: Calories 180 (Calories from Fat 90); Total Fat 10g (Saturated Fat 4.5g; Trans Fat 0.5g); Cholesterol 0mg; Sodium 90mg; Total Carbohydrate 21g (Dietary Fiber 0g; Sugars 14g); Protein 3g % Daily Value: Vitamin A 0%; Vitamin C 0%; Calcium 0%; Iron 4% Exchanges: 1/2 Starch, 1 Other Carbohydrate, 2 Fat Carbohydrate Choices: 1 1/2

pistachio bars

Prep Time: **25 minutes**   Start to Finish: **2 hours 20 minutes**   25 bars

BASE

1 cup all-purpose flour

$^1/_4$ cup sugar

$^1/_2$ cup butter or margarine

TOPPING

1 egg

$^1/_4$ cup sugar

$^1/_4$ cup corn syrup

1 tablespoon butter or
    margarine, melted

$^1/_4$ teaspoon vanilla

1 cup coarsely chopped
    pistachio nuts

$^1/_2$ cup flaked coconut

1 Heat oven to 350°F. In medium bowl, mix flour and $^1/_4$ cup sugar. With pastry blender or fork, cut in $^1/_2$ cup butter until mixture resembles coarse crumbs. Press mixture in bottom of ungreased 8-inch square pan.

2 Bake 20 to 25 minutes or until light golden brown. Cool 10 minutes.

3 Meanwhile, in medium bowl, beat egg slightly. Stir in remaining topping ingredients except pistachios and coconut until well blended. Stir in pistachios and coconut.

4 Spoon and spread pistachio mixture evenly over warm base. Bake 15 to 20 minutes longer or until edges are golden brown. Cool completely, about 1 hour 15 minutes. For bars, cut into 5 rows by 5 rows.

"Colorize" these yummy, buttery bars by using either red-dyed pistachios or natural green pistachios—or go half red and half green.

High Altitude (3500–6500 ft):
No change.

1 Bar: Calories 120 (Calories from Fat 60); Total Fat 7g (Saturated Fat 3.5g; Trans Fat 0g); Cholesterol 20mg; Sodium 40mg; Total Carbohydrate 13g (Dietary Fiber 0g; Sugars 6g); Protein 2g % Daily Value: Vitamin A 4%; Vitamin C 0%; Calcium 0%; Iron 2% Exchanges: $^1/_2$ Starch, $^1/_2$ Other Carbohydrate, 1 $^1/_2$ Fat Carbohydrate Choices: 1

cookie tartlets

Prep Time: **1 hour**   Start to Finish: **1 hour**   48 tartlets

TARTLET SHELLS

1 roll (16.5 oz) refrigerated sugar
cookies

LEMON-PISTACHIO FILLING

1 cup lemon pie filling (from
15.75-oz can)

2 tablespoons finely chopped
pistachio nuts

CHOCOLATE-ORANGE FILLING

1 cup powdered sugar

2 tablespoons unsweetened
baking cocoa

1 tablespoon butter or
margarine, softened

2 teaspoons grated orange peel

1 to 2 tablespoons orange juice

RASPBERRY CREAM FILLING

2 tablespoons cream cheese,
softened

$1/3$ cup powdered sugar

1 tablespoon seedless
raspberry jam

Fresh mint leaves or sliced
almond, if desired

1 Heat oven to 350°F. Lightly grease 24 mini muffin cups or small tart pans with shortening; sprinkle lightly with sugar. Cut half of dough into twelve $1/4$-inch slices. Keep remaining half of dough refrigerated. Cut each slice in half. Roll each half into a ball; gently press in bottom and up side of muffin cup, using floured fingers if dough is sticky. With fork, prick dough several times.

2 Bake 7 to 9 minutes or until light golden brown. Cool 10 minutes; remove from pans. Repeat with remaining dough to make 48 tartlet shells.

3 Fill tartlet shells with fillings as directed below. Store in refrigerator up to 24 hours.

4 Spoon or decoratively pipe about 1 tablespoon lemon pie filling into each of 16 tartlet shells; sprinkle pistachios over top of each.

5 In medium bowl, beat 1 cup powdered sugar, the cocoa, butter, orange peel and 1 tablespoon of the orange juice with electric mixer on low speed 1 minute or until smooth. Beat in remaining orange juice 1 teaspoon at a time just until filling is smooth and fluffy. Spoon or decoratively pipe about 2 teaspoons filling into each of 16 tartlet shells.

6 In small bowl, beat all raspberry cream filling ingredients with electric mixer on low speed 1 to 2 minutes or until light and fluffy. Spoon or decoratively pipe about 1 teaspoon filling into each of 16 tartlet shells. Garnish with mint leaves.

High Altitude (3500–6500 ft): In large bowl, break up cookie dough. Stir or knead in $1/4$ cup all-purpose flour. Bake 11 to 13 minutes.

1 Tartlet: Calories 70 (Calories from Fat 25); Total Fat 2.5g (Saturated Fat 1g; Trans Fat 0g); Cholesterol 0mg; Sodium 45mg; Total Carbohydrate 11g (Dietary Fiber 0g; Sugars 8g); Protein 0g % Daily Value: Vitamin A 0%; Vitamin C 0%; Calcium 0%; Iron 0% Exchanges: 1 Other Carbohydrate, $1/2$ Fat Carbohydrate Choices: 1

peppermint whoopie pies

Prep Time: **45 minutes**	Start to Finish: **1 Hour 25 Minutes**	24 sandwich cookies

COOKIES

1 cup granulated sugar

$^1/_2$ cup butter or margarine, softened

1 teaspoon vanilla

1 egg

1 cup milk

2 cups all-purpose flour

$^1/_2$ cup unsweetened baking cocoa

1 $^1/_2$ teaspoons baking soda

$^1/_2$ teaspoon baking powder

$^1/_2$ teaspoon salt

FILLING

3 cups powdered sugar

1 jar (7 oz) marshmallow creme

6 tablespoons butter or margarine, softened

6 tablespoons shortening

5 to 6 teaspoons milk

1 $^1/_2$ teaspoons vanilla

6 drops red food color, if desired

DECORATION

Crushed candy canes or other candies, if desired

1 Heat oven to 375°F. Grease cookie sheets with shortening or cooking spray. In large bowl, beat granulated sugar, $^1/_2$ cup butter, 1 teaspoon vanilla and the egg with electric mixer on medium speed until well blended. Stir in 1 cup milk (mixture will look curdled). Stir in remaining cookie ingredients.

2 Drop dough by rounded tablespoonfuls 2 inches apart onto cookie sheets.

3 Bake 7 to 9 minutes or until edges appear set. Cool 1 minute; remove cookies to cooling rack. Cool completely.

4 In large bowl, beat all filling ingredients on medium speed about 2 minutes or until light and fluffy. Place flat sides of 2 cookies together with 2 tablespoons filling, sandwich-style. Sprinkle edges of filling with crushed candy. Store in tightly covered container.

The irrepressible gooey-filled sandwich cookies with the whimsical name, Whoopie Pies are impossible to resist! Freeze sandwich cookies on a cookie sheet, then wrap individually in plastic wrap and toss into a resealable plastic freezer bag—they taste great straight from the freezer.

Pictured on cover.

High Altitude (3500–6500 ft): No change.

1 Sandwich Cookie: Calories 260 (Calories from Fat 100); Total Fat 11g (Saturated Fat 5g, Trans Fat 1g); Cholesterol 30mg; Sodium 200mg; Total Carbohydrate 39g (Dietary Fiber 0g, Sugars 29g); Protein 2g % Daily Value: Vitamin A 4%; Vitamin C 0%; Calcium 2%; Iron 4% Exchanges: $^1/_2$ Starch, 2 Other Carbohydrate, 2 Fat Carbohydrate Choices: 2 $^1/_2$

tin roof fudge tart

Prep Time: **1 hour**   Start to Finish: **3 hours 30 minutes**   12 servings

CRUST

1 refrigerated pie crust (from 15-oz box), softened as directed on box

2 oz dark chocolate candy bar or semisweet baking chocolate, cut into pieces

1 tablespoon butter or margarine

PEANUT LAYER

20 caramels (6 oz), unwrapped

$^1/_3$ cup whipping cream

1 $^1/_2$ cups Spanish peanuts

MOUSSE LAYER

8 oz dark chocolate candy bar or semisweet baking chocolate, cut into pieces

2 tablespoons butter or margarine

1 cup whipping cream

2 teaspoons vanilla

TOPPING

5 caramels, unwrapped

3 tablespoons whipping cream

1 teaspoon butter or margarine

Whipped cream, if desired

Spanish peanuts, if desired

1 Heat oven to 450°F. Make pie crust as directed on box for One-Crust Baked Shell using 10-inch tart pan with removable bottom or 9-inch glass pie plate. Place crust in pie plate; press in bottom and up side. Trim edge if necessary. Bake 9 to 11 minutes or until lightly browned. Cool completely, about 30 minutes.

2 In 1-quart heavy saucepan, melt 2 oz dark chocolate and 1 tablespoon butter over very low heat, stirring constantly, until smooth. Spread in bottom and up side of cooled baked shell. Refrigerate until chocolate is set, about 10 minutes.

3 Meanwhile, in 2-quart saucepan, melt 20 caramels with $^1/_3$ cup whipping cream over low heat, stirring frequently, until mixture is smooth. Stir in 1 $^1/_2$ cups peanuts until well coated; immediately spoon into chocolate-lined crust.

4 In 1-quart heavy saucepan, melt 8 oz dark chocolate and 2 tablespoons butter over very low heat, stirring constantly, until smooth. Cool slightly, about 10 minutes. In small bowl, beat 1 cup whipping cream and vanilla with electric mixer on high speed until soft peaks form. Fold $^1/_3$ of the whipped cream into chocolate mixture; fold in remaining whipped cream. Spread over peanut layer. Refrigerate until set, about 2 hours.

5 In 1-quart heavy saucepan, melt all topping ingredients over very low heat, stirring frequently, until smooth. Remove side of pan. Pipe or spoon whipped cream around edge of tart; drizzle with topping and sprinkle with peanuts. Store in refrigerator.

High Altitude (3500–6500 ft): No change.

1 Serving: Calories 520 (Calories from Fat 320); Total Fat 35g (Saturated Fat 17g; Trans Fat 0g); Cholesterol 45mg; Sodium 210mg; Total Carbohydrate 41g (Dietary Fiber 3g; Sugars 23g); Protein 8g % Daily Value: Vitamin A 8%; Vitamin C 0%; Calcium 6%; Iron 6% Exchanges: $^1/_2$ Starch, 2 Other Carbohydrate, 1 High-Fat Meat, 5 $^1/_2$ Fat Carbohydrate Choices: 3

chocolate silk raspberry tart

Prep Time: **35 minutes**	Start to Finish: **5 hours**	12 servings

20 creme-filled vanilla sandwich
cookies, crushed (2 cups)

$^1/_4$ cup butter or margarine,
melted

1 $^1/_2$ cups semisweet
chocolate chips

2 cups whipping cream

1 teaspoon vanilla

1 package (8 oz) cream cheese,
softened

1 cup fresh raspberries

2 tablespoons seedless
raspberry jam

Any flavored sandwich
cookie can be used in the
crust of this rich dessert.

1 Heat oven to 375°F. In medium bowl, mix crushed cookies
and butter. In 9- or 10-inch springform pan, press mixture in
bottom and 1 inch up side. Bake 7 to 9 minutes or until set. Cool
completely, about 30 minutes.

2 Meanwhile, in 1-quart saucepan, heat chocolate chips and $^1/_2$ cup
of the whipping cream over low heat, stirring frequently, until
chocolate is melted. Stir in vanilla. Cool to room temperature,
about 15 minutes.

3 In large bowl, beat cream cheese with electric mixer on medium
speed until smooth. Beat in chocolate mixture until creamy.
Set aside.

4 In another large bowl, beat remaining 1 $^1/_2$ cups whipping cream
with electric mixer on high speed until stiff peaks form. Fold half
of whipped cream into cream cheese mixture until blended. Fold
in remaining whipped cream. Spoon into cooled baked crust.
Refrigerate until set, about 4 hours.

5 To serve, arrange raspberries around edge of tart. In small
microwavable bowl, microwave jam on High 1 to 2 minutes,
stirring every 30 seconds, until melted; brush over raspberries.
Remove side of pan. Cut tart into wedges. Store in refrigerator.

High Altitude (3500–6500 ft):
No change.

1 Serving: Calories 430 (Calories from Fat 300); Total Fat 33g (Saturated Fat 19g; Trans Fat 1.5g); Cholesterol 75mg;
Sodium 160mg; Total Carbohydrate 29g (Dietary Fiber 2g; Sugars 18g); Protein 4g % Daily Value: Vitamin A 15%; Vitamin C
2%; Calcium 6%; Iron 8% Exchanges: 1 Starch, 1 Other Carbohydrate, 6 $^1/_2$ Fat Carbohydrate Choices: 2

coconut-lemon cream tartlets

Prep Time: **1 hour**   Start to Finish: **1 hour**   8 tartlets

²/₃ cup flaked coconut

1 box (15 oz) refrigerated pie
   crusts, softened as
   directed on box

8 individual foil tart pans
   (4 ¹/₂ × 1 ¹/₄ inch)*

2 teaspoons sugar

1 ¹/₂ cups whipping cream

1 jar (10 oz) lemon curd (1 cup)

¹/₂ cup fresh raspberries,
   if desired

1 Heat oven to 350°F. Spread coconut evenly on ungreased cookie sheet. Bake 7 to 8 minutes, stirring occasionally, until light golden brown. Increase oven temperature to 450°F.

2 Remove crusts from pouches; unroll on work surface. With rolling pin, roll each crust lightly to form 12-inch round. Using upside-down foil tart pan as guide, cut four 5-inch rounds from each crust.

3 Reserve 2 tablespoons toasted coconut for topping. Sprinkle each pie-crust round with about 1 tablespoon of the remaining coconut and ¹/₄ teaspoon sugar; roll in lightly with rolling pin. Press each round, coconut side up, in bottom and up side of tart pan. Prick bottoms and sides with fork. Place pans on large cookie sheet.

4 Bake 7 to 9 minutes or until edges are light golden brown. Cool completely, about 15 minutes.

5 In large bowl, beat whipping cream until stiff peaks form. In medium bowl, place 2 cups of the whipped cream; fold in lemon curd until well combined. Spoon into cooled baked tart shells. Top each with dollop of remaining whipped cream. Garnish with fresh raspberries and reserved coconut. To serve, gently slide tarts out of pans; place on individual dessert plates. Store in refrigerator.

*Look for the foil pans with the other disposable baking pans, or sometimes they're stocked next to the ready-made graham cracker crusts.

High Altitude (3500–6500 ft):
No change.

1 Tartlet: Calories 480 (Calories from Fat 260); Total Fat 29g (Saturated Fat 16g; Trans Fat 0g); Cholesterol 80mg; Sodium 240mg; Total Carbohydrate 51g (Dietary Fiber 0g; Sugars 27g); Protein 1g % Daily Value: Vitamin A 10%; Vitamin C 0%; Calcium 4%; Iron 0% Exchanges: ¹/₂ Starch, 3 Other Carbohydrate, 6 Fat Carbohydrate Choices: 3 ¹/₂

raspberry mirror cake

| Prep Time: **50 minutes** | Start to Finish: **2 hours 15 minutes** | 12 servings |

CAKE

1 box (1 lb 2.25 oz) white cake
   mix with pudding

1 $^1/_4$ cups water

$^1/_3$ cup vegetable oil

3 egg whites

$^1/_3$ cup seedless raspberry
   preserves

FROSTING

$^1/_2$ cup shortening

$^1/_2$ cup butter, softened

1 lb powdered sugar (about
   4 cups)

2 to 3 tablespoons kirsch or
   1 teaspoon almond or vanilla
   extract plus milk to equal
   2 to 3 tablespoons

TOPPING

$^2/_3$ cup frozen raspberry-
   cranberry blend juice
   concentrate, thawed

4 teaspoons cornstarch

1 cup fresh raspberries

Fresh mint sprigs, if desired

1 Heat oven to 350°F (if using dark or nonstick pans, heat oven to 325°F). Grease two 9-inch round cake pans with shortening; lightly flour. In large bowl, beat cake mix, water, oil and egg whites with electric mixer on low speed 30 seconds or until blended. Beat on medium speed 2 minutes, scraping bowl occasionally. Pour batter into pans.

2 Bake 23 to 28 minutes or until cake springs back when touched lightly in center. Cool in pans on cooling racks 15 minutes. Remove cakes from pans; cool completely, about 30 minutes. Stir raspberry preserves until smooth; cover and set aside.

3 Meanwhile, in large bowl, beat shortening and butter with electric mixer on medium speed until creamy. Add powdered sugar; beat until smooth. Beat in 2 tablespoons kirsch. Beat in additional kirsch if necessary for soft spreading consistency. Set aside.

4 To assemble cake, trim cake layers to even off. Place 1 cake layer, trimmed side down, on serving plate. Spread with $^1/_2$ cup frosting. Spread evenly with raspberry preserves. Top with remaining cake layer, trimmed side down. Spread top with $^1/_2$ cup frosting, smoothing top to form flat surface. Reserve $^1/_2$ cup frosting for piping. Spread side with remaining frosting.

5 Place reserved frosting in small decorating bag fitted with small star tip. Pipe decorative edge around top and bottom edge of cake.

6 In small saucepan, mix juice concentrate and cornstarch. Heat to boiling over medium-low heat, stirring constantly, until thickened. Remove from heat. Cool until thickened mixture is room temperature, about 10 minutes. Spoon on top of cake. Spread to piped edges of frosting. Before serving, arrange raspberries around top edge of cake. Garnish with mint sprigs.

High Altitude (3500–6500 ft): Follow High
Altitude directions on cake mix box.

1 Serving: Calories 600 (Calories from Fat 240); Total Fat 26g (Saturated Fat 9g; Trans Fat 3g); Cholesterol 20mg; Sodium 310mg; Total Carbohydrate 87g (Dietary Fiber 0g; Sugars 66g); Protein 3g % Daily Value: Vitamin A 4%; Vitamin C 15%; Calcium 6%; Iron 6% Exchanges: 1 Starch, 5 Other Carbohydrate, 5 Fat Carbohydrate Choices: 6

rich and easy tiramisu dessert

Prep Time: **25 minutes**　　　　Start to Finish: **5 hours 15 minutes**　　　15 servings

CAKE

¹/₄ cup butter or margarine

¹/₄ cup milk

2 eggs

³/₄ cup granulated sugar

³/₄ cup all-purpose flour

1 teaspoon baking powder

¹/₄ teaspoon salt

¹/₄ teaspoon vanilla

³/₄ cup hot strong brewed coffee

1 tablespoon granulated sugar

TOPPING

1 package (8 oz) cream cheese, softened

1 container (8 oz) mascarpone cheese or cream cheese, softened

¹/₃ cup powdered sugar

2 tablespoons Marsala wine, dark rum or cold strong brewed coffee

1 pint (2 cups) whipping cream

Grated semisweet baking chocolate (about ¹/₂ oz)

1 Heat oven to 375°F. Spray 13 × 9-inch pan with cooking spray. In small saucepan or 2-cup microwavable measuring cup, heat butter and milk until steaming hot (about 1 minute on High in microwave).

2 Meanwhile, in large bowl, beat eggs with electric mixer on high speed until light. Gradually beat in ³/₄ cup granulated sugar; beat 2 minutes longer. Add flour, baking powder, salt, vanilla and hot milk mixture; beat on low speed until smooth. Pour batter into pan.

3 Bake 14 to 16 minutes or until cake springs back when touched lightly in center. In 1-cup measuring cup, mix coffee and 1 tablespoon granulated sugar. Drizzle over warm cake. Cool completely, about 30 minutes.

4 In large bowl, beat cream cheese and mascarpone cheese with electric mixer on medium speed until smooth and creamy. Beat in powdered sugar and wine.

5 In large bowl, beat whipping cream with electric mixer until stiff peaks form. Fold into cream cheese mixture until combined. Spread evenly on cake. Sprinkle grated chocolate over top of cake. Cover; refrigerate at least 4 hours or overnight. To serve, cut into squares. Store in refrigerator.

For a shortcut version, skip baking the cake and use ladyfingers instead. Purchase two 3-ounce packages and layer ladyfingers from one package in bottom of baking pan. Drizzle ladyfingers with half of coffee mixture; spread with half of topping. Cover topping with remaining ladyfingers. Drizzle ladyfingers with remaining coffee mixture; spread with remaining topping. Continue as directed.

High Altitude (3500–6500 ft): Increase flour to 1 cup.

1 Serving: Calories 330 (Calories from Fat 220); Total Fat 25g (Saturated Fat 15g; Trans Fat 1g); Cholesterol 105mg; Sodium 200mg; Total Carbohydrate 21g (Dietary Fiber 0g; Sugars 16g); Protein 5g % Daily Value: Vitamin A 15%; Vitamin C 0%; Calcium 8%; Iron 4% Exchanges: ¹/₂ Starch, 1 Other Carbohydrate, ¹/₂ High-Fat Meat, 4 Fat Carbohydrate Choices: 1 ¹/₂

tres leches cake

Prep Time: **30 minutes**   Start to Finish: **4 hours**   15 servings

CAKE

1 box (1 lb 2.25 oz) yellow cake
    mix with pudding

1 cup water

$^1/_3$ cup vegetable oil

3 eggs

SAUCE

1 cup whipping cream

$^1/_3$ cup rum or 1 teaspoon rum
    extract plus $^1/_3$ cup water

1 can (14 oz) sweetened
    condensed milk (not
    evaporated)

1 can (12 oz) evaporated milk

TOPPING

1 cup whipping cream

$^1/_3$ cup coconut, toasted*

$^1/_3$ cup chopped macadamia nuts

1 Heat oven to 350°F. Grease 13 × 9-inch (2-quart) glass baking dish. In large bowl, beat cake mix, water, oil and eggs with electric mixer on low speed 30 seconds or until blended. Beat on medium speed 2 minutes, scraping bowl occasionally. Pour batter into baking dish. Bake 25 to 35 minutes or until toothpick inserted in center comes out clean.

2 Meanwhile, in large bowl, blend all sauce ingredients. Using long-tined fork or regular fork, pierce hot cake in baking dish every 1 to 2 inches. Slowly pour sauce mixture over cake. Refrigerate cake at least 3 hours to chill. (Cake will absorb most of sauce mixture.)

3 Before serving, in small bowl, beat 1 cup whipping cream until stiff peaks form. Spread over cold cake. Sprinkle with coconut and macadamia nuts. Store in refrigerator.

*To toast coconut, spread on cookie sheet; bake in 350°F oven 7 to 8 minutes, stirring occasionally, until light golden brown.

Tres Leches Cake is a classic Nicaraguan cake soaked with three forms of leches, or "milks." It is a very moist cake and becomes more flavorful as it's stored. Refrigerate it tightly covered up to 3 days.

High Altitude (3500–6500 ft):
No change.

1 Serving: Calories 440 (Calories from Fat 220); Total Fat 24g (Saturated Fat 11g; Trans Fat 1g); Cholesterol 90mg; Sodium 320mg; Total Carbohydrate 47g (Dietary Fiber 0g; Sugars 35g); Protein 7g % Daily Value: Vitamin A 10%; Vitamin C 0%; Calcium 20%; Iron 6% Exchanges: 1 Starch, 2 Other Carbohydrate, $^1/_2$ High-Fat Meat, 4 Fat Carbohydrate Choices: 3

key lime cream torte

Prep Time: **35 minutes**   Start to Finish: **4 hours 35 minutes**   12 servings

CAKE

1 box (1 lb 2.25 oz) butter recipe
   yellow cake mix with pudding
2 tablespoons lime juice plus
   water to equal 1 1/4 cups
1/2 cup butter, softened
3 eggs

FILLING

1 can (14 oz) sweetened
   condensed milk (not
   evaporated)
1/2 cup lime juice
2 cups whipping cream

GARNISH

Lime slices

Key lime isn't just for pie anymore. Has this flavor ever taken off—you can even order a key lime martini!

The key lime here comes in the form of creamy layers of frosting and lime-spiked cake. It's so good.

1 Heat oven to 350°F (if using dark or nonstick pans, heat oven to 325°F). Grease two 9- or 8-inch round cake pans with shortening; lightly flour. In large bowl, beat all cake ingredients with electric mixer on low speed 30 seconds or until moistened; beat on medium speed 2 minutes, scraping bowl occasionally. Pour batter evenly into pans.

2 Bake 9-inch pans 27 to 32 minutes; 8-inch pans 32 to 37 minutes or until toothpick inserted in center comes out clean. Cool 15 minutes. Remove from pans. Cool completely, about 1 hour.

3 In small bowl, mix condensed milk and 1/2 cup lime juice until well blended. In large bowl, beat whipping cream with electric mixer on high speed until stiff peaks form. Reserve 1 cup of the whipped cream. Fold condensed milk mixture into remaining whipped cream just until blended.

4 To assemble torte, cut each cake layer in half horizontally to make 4 layers. Place 1 layer, cut side up, on serving plate. Spread with 1/3 of the whipped cream filling. Repeat with second and third cake layers. Top with remaining cake layer. Pipe on decorative pattern or spread reserved whipped cream over top of torte. Refrigerate at least 2 hours before serving. Garnish with lime slices. Store in refrigerator.

High Altitude (3500–6500 ft):
No change.

1 Serving: Calories 490 (Calories from Fat 240); Total Fat 27g (Saturated Fat 16g; Trans Fat 1.5g); Cholesterol 130mg; Sodium 410mg; Total Carbohydrate 56g (Dietary Fiber 0g; Sugars 40g); Protein 6g % Daily Value: Vitamin A 15%; Vitamin C 6%; Calcium 20%; Iron 6% Exchanges: 2 Starch, 1 1/2 Other Carbohydrate, 5 Fat Carbohydrate Choices: 4

strawberry brownie mousse torte

Prep Time: **20 minutes**	Start to Finish: **4 hours 30 minutes**	16 servings

BASE

1 box (1 lb 3.8 oz) fudge brownie
  mix

$^1/_2$ cup miniature semisweet
  chocolate chips

$^1/_2$ cup vegetable oil

$^1/_4$ cup water

2 eggs

TOPPING

2 tablespoons water

1 tablespoon unflavored gelatin
  (about 1 $^1/_2$ envelopes)

1 bag (16 oz) frozen whole
  strawberries, thawed

1 $^1/_2$ cups whipping cream

$^1/_2$ cup powdered sugar

Chocolate curls, if desired

Strawberries, if desired

Fresh mint leaves, if desired

1 Heat oven to 350°F. Grease bottom only of 10-inch springform pan with shortening. In large bowl, beat all base ingredients 50 strokes with spoon. Spread in pan. Bake 35 to 40 minutes. Cool completely, about 1 $^1/_2$ hours.

2 Meanwhile, in medium saucepan, place 2 tablespoons water; sprinkle gelatin over water. Let stand 1 minute to soften. In food processor bowl with metal blade or blender, place strawberries. Cover; process until smooth. Add to softened gelatin; mix well. Cook over medium heat until gelatin is completely dissolved. Cover; refrigerate until mixture is slightly thickened, about 1 $^1/_2$ hours.

3 In large bowl, beat whipping cream and powdered sugar until stiff peaks form. Fold in strawberry mixture. Spoon over cooled brownie base. Refrigerate until set, about 2 hours. Just before serving, garnish torte with chocolate curls, strawberries, and mint leaves. Store in refrigerator.

Ring in the New Year with this smashing dessert. For another garnishing idea, how about dipping whole fresh strawberries into melted chocolate and arranging them on top of the torte?

High Altitude (3500–6500 ft): Follow High Altitude directions on brownie mix box. Bake 38 to 43 minutes.

1 Serving: Calories 330 (Calories from Fat 160); Total Fat 18g (Saturated Fat 7g; Trans Fat 1g); Cholesterol 50mg; Sodium 140mg; Total Carbohydrate 40g (Dietary Fiber 0g; Sugars 30g); Protein 3g % Daily Value: Vitamin A 6%; Vitamin C 15%; Calcium 6%; Iron 8% Exchanges: 1 Starch, 1 $^1/_2$ Other Carbohydrate, 3 $^1/_2$ Fat Carbohydrate Choices: 2 $^1/_2$

chocolate cheesecake

Prep Time: **15 minutes**   Start to Finish: **7 hours 20 minutes**   16 servings

CRUST

1 package (9 oz) thin chocolate
   wafer cookies, crushed
   (1 $^3/_4$ cups)

6 tablespoons butter or
   margarine, melted

FILLING

2 packages (8 oz each) cream
   cheese, softened

$^2/_3$ cup sugar

3 eggs

1 bag (12 oz) semisweet
   chocolate chips (2 cups),
   melted

1 cup whipping cream

2 tablespoons butter or
   margarine, melted

1 teaspoon vanilla

1 Heat oven to 325°F. In medium bowl, mix crust ingredients; reserve 1 tablespoon crumbs for garnish. Press remaining crumbs in bottom and 2 inches up side of ungreased 10-inch springform pan. Refrigerate.

2 In large bowl, beat cream cheese and sugar until smooth. Beat in 1 egg at a time until well blended. Add melted chocolate; beat well. Add remaining filling ingredients; beat until smooth. Pour into crust-lined pan.

3 Bake 55 to 65 minutes or until edges are set; center of cheesecake will be soft. (To minimize cracking, place shallow pan half full of hot water on lower oven rack during baking.) Cool in pan 5 minutes.

4 Carefully remove side of pan. Cool completely, about 2 hours. Garnish with reserved crumbs. Refrigerate at least 4 hours or overnight. Store in refrigerator.

Chocolate and cheesecake—can't go wrong with that! Don't worry about the center of the cheesecake being soft when you take it out of the oven; it becomes firm as it cools. To cut cheesecake easily, dip the knife into water and clean it off after every cut.

High Altitude (3500–6500 ft): Bake 60 to 65 minutes.

1 Serving: Calories 410 (Calories from Fat 260); Total Fat 29g (Saturated Fat 17g; Trans Fat 1g); Cholesterol 105mg; Sodium 210mg; Total Carbohydrate 32g (Dietary Fiber 2g; Sugars 24g); Protein 5g % Daily Value: Vitamin A 15%; Vitamin C 0%; Calcium 6%; Iron 8% Exchanges: $^1/_2$ Starch, 1 $^1/_2$ Other Carbohydrate, $^1/_2$ High-Fat Meat, 5 Fat Carbohydrate Choices: 2

dress up dessert!

Eat dessert first, life is short—or so one saying goes! Easier than you think, these "snazzy-pizzazzy" ideas will dress up any dessert.

Ring in the New Year by writing the year or seasonal word or message on rim of dessert plates with decorating gels.

Let it glow! Push very thin candles (slightly bigger around than a toothpick) into dessert pieces. Light candles and voilà!

Skewer it! Thread fresh, small berries onto short, decorative skewers or frilly toothpicks and push into dessert.

Purchased pirouette cookies become magical when the end is dipped into melted chocolate and then into sparkling edible glitter or colored sugar. (Let chocolate set before garnishing.) Or sprinkle edible glitter directly onto cake or other dessert.

banana-eggnog bread pudding with rum sauce

| Prep Time: 25 minutes | Start to Finish: 1 hour 20 minutes | 12 servings |

PUDDING

1 loaf (1 lb) raisin bread, cut into cubes

2 medium bananas, sliced

3 $^1/_2$ cups eggnog

4 eggs

$^1/_4$ cup granulated sugar

$^1/_4$ teaspoon ground nutmeg

SAUCE

1 cup packed brown sugar

$^1/_2$ cup whipping cream

$^1/_4$ cup dark corn syrup

2 tablespoons butter or margarine

$^1/_2$ teaspoon rum extract

1 Heat oven to 350°F. Butter 13 × 9-inch (3-quart) glass baking dish. In baking dish, place half of bread cubes. Top with banana slices and remaining bread cubes. In large bowl, blend eggnog, eggs, granulated sugar and nutmeg. Pour over bread cubes. Let stand 5 minutes.

2 Bake 40 to 50 minutes or until knife inserted in center comes out clean.

3 Meanwhile, in small saucepan, cook all sauce ingredients except rum extract over medium heat, stirring constantly, until mixture boils and thickens. Reduce heat to low; simmer 5 minutes, stirring constantly. Stir in rum extract. Serve warm sauce over pudding.

The holiday spirit of eggnog makes its way into a rich bread pudding flavored with banana and nutmeg. If you don't like raisins, just use plain white bread.

High Altitude (3500–6500 ft): Bake 45 to 50 minutes.

1 Serving: Calories 360 (Calories from Fat 100); Total Fat 11g (Saturated Fat 5g; Trans Fat 0.5g); Cholesterol 145mg; Sodium 240mg; Total Carbohydrate 57g (Dietary Fiber 2g; Sugars 39g); Protein 9g % Daily Value: Vitamin A 8%; Vitamin C 0%; Calcium 15%; Iron 10% Exchanges: 1 $^1/_2$ Starch, 2 $^1/_2$ Other Carbohydrate, $^1/_2$ High-Fat Meat, 1 Fat Carbohydrate Choices: 4

apple-raspberry cookie cobbler

| Prep Time: **10 minutes** | Start to Finish: **1 hour 55 minutes** | 10 servings |

2 cans (21 oz each) apple pie
   filling with more fruit

1 bag (12 to 14 oz) frozen
   unsweetened raspberries (3
   $^1/_2$ cups)

$^1/_4$ cup sugar

1 roll (16.5 oz) refrigerated sugar
   cookies

1 cup quick-cooking oats

2 tablespoons sugar

Ice cream, if desired

1 Heat oven to 350°F. In ungreased 13 × 9-inch (3-quart) glass baking dish, mix pie filling, raspberries and $^1/_4$ cup sugar.

2 In medium bowl, break up cookie dough. Add oats; mix well. Crumble mixture evenly over fruit mixture. Sprinkle 2 tablespoons sugar over top.

3 Bake 50 to 60 minutes or until topping is golden brown. Cool slightly before serving, about 45 minutes. Serve with ice cream.

Cookie dough isn't only for cookies; it makes a great topping for your cobblers or crisps! Old-fashioned oats can be used in the topping mixture, but it will have a coarser, more crumbly texture.

High Altitude (3500–6500 ft):
No change.

1 Serving: Calories 420 (Calories from Fat 90); Total Fat 10g (Saturated Fat 2.5g; Trans Fat 2g); Cholesterol 15mg; Sodium 130mg; Total Carbohydrate 79g (Dietary Fiber 8g; Sugars 50g); Protein 4g % Daily Value: Vitamin A 0%; Vitamin C 20%; Calcium 4%; Iron 10% Exchanges: 1 Starch, 1 Fruit, 3 Other Carbohydrate, 2 Fat Carbohydrate Choices: 5

pineapple-cherry quick bread

Prep Time: **30 minutes**	Start to Finish: **2 hours 25 minutes**	2 loaves (12 slices each)

4 cups all-purpose flour

1 ¹/₂ cups granulated sugar

1 teaspoon baking soda

1 teaspoon salt

³/₄ cup vegetable oil

1 tablespoon vanilla

4 eggs

1 can (8 oz) crushed pineapple in
  unsweetened juice, undrained

1 jar (10 oz) maraschino
  cherries, quartered, well
  drained

2 teaspoons powdered sugar

1 Heat oven to 325°F. Grease bottoms only of two 8 × 4-inch loaf pans with shortening; lightly flour. In large bowl, mix flour, granulated sugar, baking soda and salt. Add oil, vanilla, eggs and pineapple with juice; mix with electric mixer on low speed until combined. Fold in cherries. Spoon batter into pans.

2 Bake 45 to 55 minutes or until toothpick inserted in center comes out clean. Cool in pans 10 minutes. Remove loaves from pans; place on cooling racks. Cool completely, about 1 hour. Sprinkle cooled loaves with powdered sugar.

For mini loaves, grease bottoms only of five 5 ³/₄ × 3 ¹/₄ × 2-inch foil loaf pans with shortening; lightly flour. Divide batter evenly into pans, using about 1 cup batter for each. Place filled pans on cookie sheet. Bake at 325°F 40 to 50 minutes or until toothpick inserted in center comes out clean.

High Altitude (3500–6500 ft): Heat oven to 350°F. Bake 8 × 4-inch pans 60 to 65 minutes; bake mini loaf pans (see tip) 40 to 50 minutes.

1 Slice: Calories 220 (Calories from Fat 70); Total Fat 8g (Saturated Fat 1.5g; Trans Fat 0g); Cholesterol 35mg; Sodium 160mg; Total Carbohydrate 35g (Dietary Fiber 1g; Sugars 18g); Protein 3g % Daily Value: Vitamin A 0%; Vitamin C 0%; Calcium 0%; Iron 6% Exchanges: ¹/₂ Starch, 2 Other Carbohydrate, 1 ¹/₂ Fat Carbohydrate Choices: 2

mushroom-garlic cream tartlets

| Prep Time: **15 minutes** | Start to Finish: **35 minutes** | 24 tartlets |

2 tablespoons butter or
   margarine

1 package (8 oz) fresh
   mushrooms, finely chopped

1 tablespoon all-purpose flour

1 tablespoon finely chopped
   onion

2 cloves garlic, finely chopped

1/2 cup whipping cream

1/4 cup grated Parmesan cheese

1 can (8 oz) refrigerated crescent
   dinner rolls

2 tablespoons chopped fresh
   parsley

1 Heat oven to 350°F. In 10-inch skillet, melt butter over medium heat. Stir in mushrooms, flour, onion and garlic. Cook 5 minutes, stirring frequently, until vegetables are tender.

2 Stir in whipping cream and cheese. Cook 2 to 3 minutes, stirring frequently, until most of liquid has evaporated.

3 Unroll dough into 2 long rectangles; firmly press perforations to seal. Cut each rectangle into 12 squares. Place 1 square in each of 24 ungreased mini muffin cups. Firmly press in bottom and up sides, leaving corners of dough extended over edges of cups. Spoon 1 heaping teaspoon mushroom mixture into each cup.

4 Bake 9 to 12 minutes or until golden brown. Sprinkle with parsley. Cool in pan 5 minutes. Remove tartlets from muffin cups; serve warm. Store in refrigerator.

Make a double batch, because these will be the first appetizers to disappear! Make the crescent dough shells and filling ahead. Cover and refrigerate them separately up to 2 hours. Fill the shells just before baking.

High Altitude (3500–6500 ft):
No change.

1 Tartlet: Calories 70 (Calories from Fat 45); Total Fat 5g (Saturated Fat 2.5g; Trans Fat 0.5g); Cholesterol 10mg; Sodium 100mg; Total Carbohydrate 5g (Dietary Fiber 0g; Sugars 1g); Protein 2g % Daily Value: Vitamin A 2%; Vitamin C 0%; Calcium 0%; Iron 0% Exchanges: 1/2 Starch, 1 Fat Carbohydrate Choices: 1/2

crescent-crab purses

Prep Time: **20 minutes** | Start to Finish: **40 minutes** | 12 appetizers

1 can (6 oz) crabmeat, well
 drained

2 tablespoons grated Parmesan
 cheese

2 tablespoons sharp process
 cheese spread (from 5-oz jar)

1 tablespoon chopped fresh
 parsley, if desired

1/8 teaspoon ground red pepper
 (cayenne)

1 clove garlic, finely chopped

1 can (8 oz) refrigerated crescent
 dinner rolls

1 Heat oven to 375°F. In small bowl, mix all ingredients except dough. Unroll dough into 1 large rectangle; press into 12 × 9-inch rectangle, firmly pressing perforations to seal. Cut rectangle into twelve 3-inch squares.

2 Place about 1 tablespoon crab mixture on each dough square. Bring all sides together in center; press to seal. With fingers, pinch dough firmly about 1/4 inch below edges, making a pouch with points extending over top. Place on ungreased cookie sheet.

3 Bake 12 to 17 minutes or until deep golden brown. Immediately remove from cookie sheet. Serve warm.

These "purses" are a take on steamed Chinese appetizer buns and resemble drawstring pouches. Pinch the dough together firmly over the filling so each "pouch" stays sealed.

High Altitude (3500–6500 ft): No change.

1 Appetizer: Calories 90 (Calories from Fat 45); Total Fat 5g (Saturated Fat 2g; Trans Fat 1g); Cholesterol 15mg; Sodium 240mg; Total Carbohydrate 8g (Dietary Fiber 0g; Sugars 2g); Protein 5g % Daily Value: Vitamin A 0%; Vitamin C 0%; Calcium 4%; Iron 2% Exchanges: 1/2 Starch, 1/2 Lean Meat, 1/2 Fat Carbohydrate Choices: 1/2

mini chicken caesar cups

Prep Time: **20 minutes**   Start to Finish: **35 minutes**   20 appetizers

1 cup finely chopped cooked
   chicken

3 tablespoons Caesar dressing

1 can (12 oz) refrigerated flaky
   or buttermilk flaky biscuits

1/4 cup finely sliced romaine
   lettuce

1 oz shaved Parmesan cheese

1 Heat oven to 400°F. In small bowl, mix chicken and dressing.

2 Separate dough into 10 biscuits; divide each into 2 rounds. Press dough rounds in bottom and up sides of 20 ungreased mini muffin cups, extending dough 1/4 inch above edge of cups. Fill each cup with about 2 teaspoons chicken mixture.

3 Bake 8 to 11 minutes or until crust is deep golden brown. Remove from cups. Top each with lettuce and cheese. Serve warm.

Use a vegetable peeler to shave the Parmesan cheese. The shavings are larger than shreds, giving you that restaurant-style look. Shredded cheese would also work.

High Altitude (3500–6500 ft): Bake 10 to 13 minutes.

1 Appetizer: Calories 80 (Calories from Fat 40); Total Fat 4.5g (Saturated Fat 1g; Trans Fat 1g); Cholesterol 5mg; Sodium 230mg; Total Carbohydrate 7g (Dietary Fiber 0g; Sugars 1g); Protein 3g % Daily Value: Vitamin A 0%; Vitamin C 0%; Calcium 0%; Iron 2% Exchanges: 1/2 Starch, 1 Fat Carbohydrate Choices: 1/2

helpful nutrition and cooking information

nutrition guidelines

We provide nutrition information for each recipe that includes calories, fat, cholesterol, sodium, carbohydrate, fiber and protein. Individual food choices can be based on this information.

Recommended intake for a daily diet of 2,000 calories as set by the Food and Drug Administration		
Total Fat	Less than 65g
Saturated Fat	Less than 20g
Cholesterol	Less than 300mg
Sodium	Less than 2,400mg
Total Carbohydrate	300g
Dietary Fiber	25g

Criteria Used for Calculating Nutrition Information

- The first ingredient was used wherever a choice is given (such as $^1/_3$ cup sour cream or plain yogurt).

- The first ingredient amount was used wherever a range is given (such as 3- to 3$^1/_2$–pound cut-up broiler-fryer chicken).

- The first serving number was used wherever a range is given (such as 4 to 6 servings).

- "If desired" ingredients and recipe variations were not included (such as sprinkle with brown sugar, if desired).

- Only the amount of a marinade or frying oil that is estimated to be absorbed by the food during preparation or cooking was calculated.

Ingredients Used in Recipe Testing and Nutrition Calculations

- Ingredients used for testing represent those that the majority of consumers use in their homes: large eggs, 2% milk, 80%-lean ground beef, canned ready-to-use chicken broth and vegetable oil spread containing not less than 65% fat.

- Fat-free, low-fat or low-sodium products were not used, unless otherwise indicated.

- Solid vegetable shortening (not butter, margarine, nonstick cooking sprays or vegetable oil spread as they can cause sticking problems) was used to grease pans, unless otherwise indicated.

Equipment Used in Recipe Testing

- We use equipment for testing that the majority of consumers use in their homes. If a specific piece of equipment (such as a wire whisk) is necessary for recipe success, it is listed in the recipe.

- Cookware and bakeware without nonstick coatings were used, unless otherwise indicated.

- No dark-colored, black or insulated bakeware was used.

- When a pan is specified in a recipe, a metal pan was used; a baking dish or pie plate means ovenproof glass was used.

- An electric hand mixer was used for mixing only when mixer speeds are specified in the recipe directions. When a mixer speed is not given, a spoon or fork was used.

Cooking Terms Glossary

Beat: Mix ingredients vigorously with spoon, fork, wire whisk, hand beater or electric mixer until smooth and uniform.

Boil: Heat liquid until bubbles rise continuously and break on the surface and steam is given off. For rolling boil, the bubbles form rapidly.

Chop: Cut into coarse or fine irregular pieces with a knife, food chopper, blender or food processor.

Cube: Cut into squares $1/2$ inch or larger.

Dice: Cut into squares smaller than $1/2$ inch.

Grate: Cut into tiny particles using small rough holes of grater (citrus peel or chocolate).

Grease: Rub the inside surface of a pan with shortening, using pastry brush, piece of waxed paper or paper towel, to prevent food from sticking during baking (as for some casseroles).

Julienne: Cut into thin, matchlike strips, using knife or food processor (vegetables, fruits, meats).

Mix: Combine ingredients in any way that distributes them evenly.

Sauté: Cook foods in hot oil or margarine over medium-high heat with frequent tossing and turning motion.

Shred: Cut into long thin pieces by rubbing food across the holes of a shredder, as for cheese, or by using a knife to slice very thinly, as for cabbage.

Simmer: Cook in liquid just below the boiling point on top of the stove; usually after reducing heat from a boil. Bubbles will rise slowly and break just below the surface.

Stir: Mix ingredients until uniform consistency. Stir once in a while for stirring occasionally, often for stirring frequently and continuously for stirring constantly.

Toss: Tumble ingredients (such as green salad) lightly with a lifting motion, usually to coat evenly or mix with another food.

metric conversion guide

volume

U.S. Units	Canadian Metric	Australian Metric
1/4 teaspoon	1 mL	1 ml
1/2 teaspoon	2 mL	2 ml
1 teaspoon	5 mL	5 ml
1 tablespoon	15 mL	20 ml
1/4 cup	50 mL	60 ml
1/3 cup	75 mL	80 ml
1/2 cup	125 mL	125 ml
2/3 cup	150 mL	170 ml
3/4 cup	175 mL	190 ml
1 cup	250 mL	250 ml
1 quart	1 liter	1 liter
1 1/2 quarts	1.5 liters	1.5 liters
2 quarts	2 liters	2 liters
2 1/2 quarts	2.5 liters	2.5 liters
3 quarts	3 liters	3 liters
4 quarts	4 liters	4 liters

weight

U.S. Units	Canadian Metric	Australian Metric
1 ounce	30 grams	30 grams
2 ounces	55 grams	60 grams
3 ounces	85 grams	90 grams
4 ounces (1/4 pound)	115 grams	125 grams
8 ounces (1/2 pound)	225 grams	225 grams
16 ounces (1 pound)	455 grams	500 grams
1 pound	455 grams	1/2 kilogram

Note: The recipes in this cookbook have not been developed or tested using metric measures. When converting recipes to metric, some variations in quality may be noted.

measurements

Inches	Centimeters
1	2.5
2	5.0
3	7.5
4	10.0
5	12.5
6	15.0
7	17.5
8	20.5
9	23.0
10	25.5
11	28.0
12	30.5
13	33.0

temperatures

Fahrenheit	Celsius
32°	0°
212°	100°
250°	120°
275°	140°
300°	150°
325°	160°
350°	180°
375°	190°
400°	200°
425°	220°
450°	230°
475°	240°
500°	260°

index

Numbers in *italics* indicate photos.